S0-FJA-041

Praise for *Hope All the Way*

"Theo Boyd brings a new, unique voice and approach to navigating grief and recovery that every generation can benefit from immediately."

—**Jason Dorsey**, Author of *Zconomy*

"Meeting Theo Boyd for our first counseling session, I was unprepared to hear the devastating losses in her life. Theo's story is well summed up by the title of her first book, *My Grief Is Not Like Yours*. Since our first meeting, I have witnessed a phoenix rising from the ashes of her life. Her latest book, *Hope All the Way*, is an inspiration of the resilience, courage, and determination of a woman whose deep faith has sustained and healed her. Anyone who is in 'the dark night of the soul' will benefit from reading this message of hope."

—**Mary Ann Cody**, MAC, LCDC, CCHT

"In *Hope All the Way*, Theo continues the journey she began in *My Grief Is Not Like Yours*, moving from the depths of loss toward the quiet strength of healing. With honesty and deep faith, she shows how hope can reappear through God's gentle signs—even in our darkest moments. This book is a heartfelt reminder that while grief never fully leaves us, neither does God."

—**Karla Pope**, Former Colleague and Lifelong Friend

"Theo Boyd's *Hope All the Way* is a tender reminder that the steadiness of hope eases the fluidity of grief. Boyd shares her personal story and struggle to shine light on the consistency of hope as a gift from a loving God who understands a difficult world. You'll be strengthened knowing that hope is abundant, available, and free to all who choose to notice its divine signs. This book will show you how!"

—**Chris Janssen**, Life Coach and National Bestselling Author of *Grace Yourself*

"I connected with Theo Boyd years ago through what seemed like a random series of events. But as I navigated my own grief, Theo's story became a guiding light—a road map for healing, as if greater forces had collaborated to connect us. Her unwavering strength and willingness to share her heart with those closest to her is matched only by her tireless efforts to offer hope to everyone through her writings. *Hope All the Way* invites us to embrace life again, knowing that hope is always waiting for us, even in the darkest of times."

—**Ron Corning**, Marketing Professional

"In *Hope All the Way,* Theo Boyd shows that there *is* hope after loss. She talks about how to appreciate the signs in everyday life from our loved ones and to find comfort in those memories."

—**Jennifer Sykora**, Teacher and Fellow Griever

HOPE ALL THE WAY

HOPE ALL THE WAY

DISCOVERING DIVINE SIGNS
in LIFE AFTER LOSS

THEO BOYD

Hope All the Way: Discovering Divine Signs in Life After Loss

All marginal stats in this book are derived from the author's research study with The Center for Generational Kinetics.

Published by Forefront Books, Nashville, Tennessee.
Distributed by Simon & Schuster.

Library of Congress Control Number: 2025943400

Print ISBN: 978-1-63763-437-0
E-book ISBN: 978-1-63763-438-7

Cover Design by Jonathan Lewis
Interior Design by PerfecType, Nashville, TN
Illustrations by Bill Kersey, KerseyGraphics

Printed in the United States of America
25 26 27 28 29 30 RR4 10 9 8 7 6 5 4 3 2 1

To the broken hearts lost in grief, this book is dedicated to you, the broken heart you carry, and the hope that fills the cracks as you heal.

CONTENTS

SPECIAL EXTRAS

ACKNOWLEDGMENTS

To the women in my life . . .

My precious daughter, Reagen,
When I think of what I'm thankful for in this life, I think of you. With the funny wit of your Grandpa "Bob" and the elegant poise of your Grandma "Nanny," you are a constant reminder of the love they poured into your life. I can see where your gentle love for animals, your passion for plants, and your joy in cooking come from—your grandparents are a beautiful part of you.

Reagen singing "Jesus Loves Me" with her Grandpa Bob, summer, 2002

I have such precious memories of you standing on top of the piano singing "Jesus Loves Me" with your Bob. You were so little and unabashed, as you sang so proudly for all to hear. Don't ever forget the words in that song. The love God has for you is the single most important ingredient in your life.

Thank you for being *you*—my daughter, my inspiration, and a source of pride for all of us. I am endlessly grateful for you.

You are hope.

I love you.

I keep seeing myself in my daughter,
and I see my mother in me and in her.
— Julie Walters

Nellene, you are the *only* reason that the farm is still running smoothly. Being the constant caretaker for a thirty-two-year-old horse is a daily and demanding task. Your patience with everything that a farm involves is comforting, and your dedication to all of us is appreciated more than you know. We are all so blessed to have you in our lives. We love you.

Shantana (Shan), I have no doubt that God brought you into my life to help my first book reach exactly who He intended—and He will do it again with this one. Thank you for always being the Shan-shine we need.

Kristi, thank you for being my biggest cheerleader, my go-to person when I need balance, and my working partner in making a difference. But most of all, thank you for being my friend.

A true friend is someone that thinks you are a good egg,
even though he knows you are slightly cracked.
—Bernard Meltzer

Kara, working through the book with you was almost like talking to my younger self. Thank you for the kind consideration you offered and for sharing your most heartfelt sympathies. I am thankful God brought you into my journey.

My fairy blonde-mothers and *all* the girlfriends who continue to magically show up in my life, I couldn't have come this far without your unwavering and unconditional support. At any moment, one of you has been there to lend an ear, offering love and understanding. The bond of friendship among women is not only powerful but essential for healing and happiness. Thank you all for your love, encouragement, and for the protection I feel when you are around—I hope you know just how deeply I treasure each of you.

A friend is like a favorite recipe—one that knows
the perfect ingredients
to lift your spirit and can always bring the right flavor back
when you've lost your taste for life.
—Author unknown

To the men in my life . . .

My love, my Ronnie Joe,
From the moment we met, I knew it was meant to be. You were the missing piece of my life, the one I was always meant to find, and now that I have you, I can't imagine living without you.

Having you by my side—standing with me, dancing with me, and loving me through this journey of ups and downs—fills my heart with joy every single day. Thank you for sharing your farm, your food, your family, and your faith with me so generously. It feels as though I've known you for a lifetime, yet I'm incredibly thankful that I get to spend the rest of it with you.

I will always love you.

It feels like home to me
It feels like home to me
It feels like I'm all the way back where I belong
—Randy Newman, "It Feels Like Home to Me"

My homebuilder, Chase,
From our very first conversation, I could feel you have a rare gift for taking dreams and transforming them into something real—through concrete, wood, and bricks. When I suggest something, you take it seriously, you believe in it, and you make it happen. You bring hope into every project with your hands, turning visions into realities.

Thank you for respecting the land and the memories it holds; for helping me find my way home again—a place where hope, renewal, and new beginnings are always possible.

Home is the nicest word there is.[1]
—from *Little House on the Prairie* television series based on the books by Laura Ingalls Wilder

My furry, faithful, and forever fearless Manly,
We've been through so much together, you and me. Your loyalty is as constant as the warmth of a home-cooked meal, and you know me better than anyone else. With you beside me for what life hands out, good or bad, I am always able to stand again. You are the anchor that keeps me from being washed away.

The love I see reflected in your eyes is a mirror to the love I carry for you in my heart, warm and comforting like the simplest, most nourishing meal. When I'm with you, the world slows down, and being fully present with you is all that matters. I will savor every moment we share, right up until the final one, and, even then, I know you'll still be with me, in heart and spirit, like a recipe passed down through the years.

To the places . . .

Bloomin' Groomin' Pet Spa & Resort,
Without you, this book would have been much harder to write. Knowing Manly was in your care during those long days of writing gave me the peace I needed to get it done. When dropping off "Mr. Part-Time," I would watch him strut in the front door to go claim his bed for the day. It would give him great purpose to show those other dogs how relaxing and playing at the daycare should be done. And let's be honest, he takes his job of relaxing *very* seriously.

You've created the perfect blend of calm and chaos to keep him happy and content. I thank God every day for Manly's daycare (and I'm pretty sure he does too). From Manly's heart and from mine, thank you for loving us.

If there are no dogs in Heaven, then when I die,
I want to go where they went.
—Will Rogers

Overflow Coffee,
With the comforting smell of coffee and peppermint tea, I feel at home inside your walls. As memories swirl and thoughts race, they begin to unravel into something more when I sit in my usual spot upstairs. The atmosphere you've created is the perfect blend of peace and inspiration, providing the foundation every writer needs to turn fleeting thoughts into something lasting. A cup of coffee or tea with a grilled cheese sandwich is the fuel that pushes me to bring my dreams to life. I am beyond grateful for this special corner of my life—a space overflowing with love, hope, and kindness!

May the God of hope fill you
with all joy and peace as you trust in him,
so that you may overflow with hope by
the power of the Holy Spirit.
Romans 15:13

NOTE TO THE READER

The information in this book is intended to be a source of encouragement based on my personal experiences with grief. This book is not intended to be used in place of therapy or other professional medical help. Please be mindful of your own mental health while reading about my journey.

INTRODUCTION

"For I know the plans I have for you," declares the Lord, "plans to prosper you and not to harm you, plans to give you hope and a future."
—Jeremiah 29:11

I NEVER ASKED FOR A miracle, until grief left me begging for one. Hope didn't come all at once—it came in flashes, in whispers, and in the silent spaces I almost overlooked.

Not very long ago, I experienced several traumatic losses—the loss of my mom to a tractor accident, the loss of my husband to another woman, the loss of my beloved therapist, and the loss of my dad to suicide—all over the span of three years. I wrote about this in detail in my previous book, *My Grief Is Not Like Yours*. If I hadn't experienced this profound grief, I don't think I would ever have given a second thought to what the world of grief looks or feels like. When you've lived through deep loss, you see life differently. You understand that grief isn't just sadness—it's love with nowhere to go.

When grief first enters your life, it can feel like a storm you aren't prepared for. You're tossed around, pulled under, sometimes gasping for air. It can feel overwhelming, unrelenting, and all-consuming. However, somewhere in that storm, you can begin to recognize the ways love continues, even beyond this life. You start to see that those you've lost carry on in some way.

I believe that those we've lost are still with us. Their presence can linger in quiet moments, subtle signs, and unexplainable occurrences. I used to wonder if I were imagining it all—the unexpected song playing at just the right time or the dream that seemed more like a memory. But after countless so-called *coincidences,* I no longer believe in that word. God doesn't do anything coincidentally. His plan is delivered with power, passion, and purpose, and that includes the years after loss and throughout our journey of healing. Every whisper of hope, every sign you see, is orchestrated with precision. I believe that if something seems like a coincidence, God is the one behind it.

When lights go out . . . a certain song plays . . . a clock stops . . . new hearts meet—these are all divine signs, glimpses of a bigger plan. Why don't we talk more about these things? Maybe it's because grief, like faith, is deeply personal. Maybe we shy away from or hesitate to talk about the signs we see and feel because we fear judgment—the skeptical glance, the polite nod, the unspoken doubt that lingers in the air, the possibility of being misunderstood.

But I think these signs are opportunities for healing. We can hold on to the moments, the signs, the feelings, the sentiments, the dreams, the soft and secret whispers, the reminders that we are never truly alone—and embrace them as the love letters they are. Love letters from those we've lost, and love letters from a God who cares for us.

During my losses, I wrote my first book as an outlet for my emotions and as a source of healing. I couldn't keep it all inside. I never would have survived! I needed to share it. And here in my second book, I have filled these pages with the tools that helped me through the hardest years of my life. The signs that shook me awake. The moments that reminded me of my purpose and the undeniable proof that love doesn't end—it simply changes form. All of these divine signs are hope all along the way as you begin to heal and live again after loss.

> 69% of grieving Americans believe signs from loved ones who have passed away are helpful in healing.

I lost my faith for a time when my grief began, but the beauty of hope is that it can be found in little moments; it's always there. Hope is the thread that stitches us back

HOPE—A Way for Renewal

H—Harvest faith and strength from your struggles.
O—Open your heart to new beginnings.
P—Preserve the love and lessons from the past.
E—Enjoy the sweetness of the journey, even after the bitter days.

together when we feel torn apart. It's the missing ingredient for a recipe to live again. It comes in the form of a friend who calls at the perfect time, or it shows up in our mailbox when we receive a sweet card from a person who cares.

What is it about this four-letter word that keeps us going? With hope, we enter another world. Even though we may still experience chaos and darkness, as we start to heal, we'll see rays of light breaking through the hardened black paint. Those rays of light are hope shining for you, guiding you, leading you. Once you start to see divine signs in the little moments, you can use those bits of light to move forward.

Whenever I see bales of hay scattered in an open field, I see Daddy feeding the cows, and I see hope. Whenever I bake in the kitchen, I see glimpses of Momma, and I feel hope. And whenever I order a steak or eat eggs, it reminds me of the new love I found, and I understand hope. Because food—particularly steak and eggs—have been such important signs for me, I've organized the book using chapter titles that describe different ways you can prepare steak and eggs. (And yes, the chapters do all relate to grief and healing.)

Wherever you start to see divine signs in the months and years after your loss, know that hope is there. It may be subtle, like a caterpillar waiting patiently in its cocoon. But once it emerges and takes flight, you can ride its wings into a bright and beautiful future.

1

Raw

The rawness of our reality is the fuel for our faith.
—Theo Boyd

We need to X-ray it and make sure nothing's broken," the doctor said before he quickly left the room for another emergency down the hall.

How can this be happening? Is the world crashing in around me, or am I crashing into it? Momma's funeral was in three days, and I had so many things to take care of, so much preparation that needed to be done. The reality of her death was still so raw, and a silly accident had brought me here to the hospital just days after Momma's horrific death.

I had run into a plow. I knew not to drive the ATV so fast through that field. Daddy had so much old equipment scattered around, and much of it hadn't been used for years, so the grass and weeds had grown tall around everything. Despite that, I'd driven through the field as fast as my emotions were running, full speed ahead, with no limit to my feelings of desperation. I needed to escape everything, all of it. I needed to breathe the air and feel like I was in control of something, anything. Unfortunately, my recklessness had driven me right into a plow and landed me in the emergency room.

As I lay there on the white sheet covering the gurney, I noticed the kitchen towel I'd wrapped around my arm was not really doing the trick anymore. In addition to the blood splatter on my shirt and pants, I was starting to bleed onto the sheets underneath me. I lifted the towel to readjust it, exposing my injured elbow. I could see blood still oozing out of my gaping flesh, but I didn't feel anything. It was numb. I was numb. All over.

With the nightmare of Momma's death still playing out in my mind, I lay there working hard to keep my thoughts straight. *I just bought these pants. Now they're ruined. I don't think I can get these stains out. Maybe Momma . . .* I closed my eyes tightly, realizing what I'd just thought. As I slowly opened them, I wanted to see something different in front of me, a different reality, but the scene was only changing from bad to worse. Even though the room they had put me in was glaringly white and bright, I was in a very dark place.

The nurse came in to take my vitals—blood pressure, body temperature, pulse. I could have told her not to bother, as I was sure they were all through the roof.

"My mom just died. The funeral is this Saturday. I really need to get back to my dad," I said, hoping she would sense my urgency and speed things along.

"Oh, I'm sorry," she replied in a somewhat routine-sounding voice.

"Daddy ran over her with one of the tractors on our farm," I blurted out. I felt like screaming it down the halls, so that everyone would know that the most phenomenal creature on the planet was gone, and her surviving husband was living in hell on earth, in a state of constant agony and torment over the accident that had happened just three days before.

"Oh my gosh, that's you? That was your mother? I heard it on the scanner here." Her businesslike manner was quickly replaced with deep compassion. I hadn't told her this to gain sympathy. I just needed her to understand my urgency by letting her know how much I had on my plate. My plate. Daddy's plate. *I need to get back and make sure Daddy has something to eat.* Momma was gone, and she was the one who had cooked all their meals. *What is he going to do?* To the best of my knowledge, besides breakfast, Daddy was capable of making only a meal of canned pork and beans, sardines with saltine crackers, and a Moon Pie.

Five hours and nine stitches later, I arrived back at the farm, only to find a house full of people from the community and beyond, visiting with Daddy, comforting him.

"Nothing's broken, just busted," I announced, all eyes focusing on my elbow as I walked in the front door.

"Oh, honey, I'm so sorry," Daddy moaned as he hugged me.

I didn't need him worrying about anything as small as my elbow right now.

"I'm fine, Daddy, really. It doesn't hurt at all," I lied. My arm was throbbing in the L-shaped position the doctor had set it in.

As I turned to look in the kitchen, I saw . . . food! There was so much food. It looked like the feeding of the five thousand from the Bible story. I hadn't seen that much tinfoil since Daddy had helped me with my seventh-grade science project.

This worry I'd had while in the emergency room was gone, completely—at least for now. I felt relief knowing that Daddy and the family would have food, good food that had been prepared by country cooks, farmers, our friends and neighbors. I could take that concern off my plate. In her way, Momma was there. She was taking care of us with food from friends and family who were giving back small portions of the love she had always shown them.

Could food be a sign?

I didn't recognize it at first, but looking back, food was the first sure sign that Momma was okay, and she was making sure we were too. God provides for those who are in need when they lean on Him. I was leaning so hard in the other direction that I was falling apart and driving into plows. But nourishment had been provided to help us stay strong in the days ahead.

Grief is a raw experience. Any part of life that once seemed ordinary becomes sensitive to the touch, and any advice given can feel like salt poured in an open wound. In grief, I felt like someone had peeled back all my layers, and all my pain receptors were completely open to the elements, exposed to the cruel world. I was feeling too much, the pain arriving in ways I never knew were possible—physically, emotionally, and spiritually. My pain threshold was low, and my sense of self was even lower. *What is the purpose of this pain?* My emotions were as raw as my busted and bloody arm.

Daddy needed me. My daughter, Reagen, needed me. And I needed something—anything—to pull me out of the sadness I was drowning in. I wasn't just searching for healing; I was desperate for it, craving it. Wanting to feel something other than the constant, gnawing sadness that seemed to follow me like a shadow. My faith, once steady, was slipping through my fingers like flour sifting into a bowl—too fine to hold, too light to grasp. I had no idea how to fix it, how to get back to the life I recognized. All I knew was that it felt like a distant memory—a forgotten recipe where some of the ingredients were missing, and the cooking steps were so foggy that I couldn't quite recall the details.

I wanted to go back to that past, pre-grief, a life filled with color, radiance, and warmth. But how could I find my way back when the path ahead was blinding me? The light that used to guide me now seemed *too* bright, turning the world into a place I struggled to recognize, and all I felt like doing was shutting my eyes. I needed a strong guide to help me see the path ahead without blinding me in the process. I needed to look up. I didn't want the light to go away, but I wasn't ready to see it in its entirety.

> 75% of grieving Americans state it was difficult for them to face the reality of the situation after their most recent grief experience.

Reality hit me in the form of 782 people paying their respects at Momma's funeral visitation. I knew there would be a crowd, but I never dreamed we would stand and hug people in what looked like an assembly line for over three hours. Each time I looked up toward the back of the chapel, I never saw a break in the line.

My feet were hurting from the constant standing, my back was in pain from leaning over to hold Daddy from time to time, and my head never stopped pounding.

I ignored the words of the ER doctor: "Don't move your arm out of this position, or the stitches may break." After the visitation, several people let me know that the dressing on my elbow was leaking. In an attempt to disguise the wound, I'd wrapped an Ace bandage around the white gauze that hugged my right elbow. I didn't have the strength to talk about anything beyond the obvious reason why we were all there.

We left the funeral home that evening later than expected, and I drove myself back to the hospital alone. The sky was filling fast with clouds, and darkness came quickly. I'd sent Daddy with family who would take him home, and then I walked back into the same ER I'd visited just a few days earlier. Thankfully, it wasn't a busy Friday night, so they were able to get me right back in—same room, same nurse, same doctor.

"I think I may need you to look at my stitches," I said, as if I were a small child about to receive punishment for not obeying.

"No problem, let's get you stitched back up."

That's all we want, isn't it? To be stitched back up. *Someone, please take this broken, torn-up, crumbling mess. Stitch it up, heal it, and make it whole again.* I was desperate to find a way back to where I'd been before all this happened, to something I could recognize, something familiar, something that reminded me of home.

Oh, how I had longed for Momma during this ordeal. We all want our moms when we are hurting, scared, or sick. I was so distracted by my pain that I didn't realize she was there. She was in the room with me. She was in the air around me. Her love was in the bandage wrapped around my elbow. Her arms were hugging me, letting me know she was there, but it was all too fresh for me to feel beyond my pain. It wasn't until years later that I was able to reflect and see the beauty in everything that had happened that week.

You are going to have the light just a little while longer . . .
—John 12:35

It was the Saturday of Momma's funeral, which was scheduled for 11:00 a.m. We would have visitors over to the house after the cemetery service. This was what Daddy wanted, so my sister and I coordinated with friends and family to get some barbecue and all the fixings delivered to the house while we were at the funeral.

I put Momma's new bedspread on their bed. Daddy said she had been waiting to put in on because she wanted to surprise me and my sister when we came to visit. He suggested I get it out now so that, when family and friends came over after the funeral, they could see Momma and Daddy's bed all made up with the new, pretty cover.

Just a few days before the accident, Momma and Daddy had gone to Walmart in town to purchase some bedding. Daddy said she'd taken her time while he waited for her, sitting in his usual spot on the small bench at the front of the store by the greeter. After a little while, she found the perfect bedspread. She always wanted Daddy's approval before she made a purchase, and he agreed that it was "really pretty . . . beautiful."

Momma loved a pretty bedroom. She always took such pride in her home, making sure things were spick-and-span. I often thought she was a little too obsessed with housework. We hear people say they're doing their spring cleaning, but Momma's was spring, summer, fall, winter, and every day in between. Every time I smell Pine-Sol (from the original yellow bottle), I am taken back to my childhood bedroom and bathroom.

The bedspread *was* beautiful. Daddy and I both stood and admired it. He was crying a little but trying to hold himself together for what the morning had in store.

As we were preparing to leave the house, Daddy wanted to make sure I'd turned off all the lights. This was a routine I had become accustomed to from an early age. "Turn off the lights! Unplug all your hair curlers!" We could never leave the house until Daddy checked all the plugs and light switches, and I inherited his paranoia of second-guessing what had been left on or off.

As I made my rounds, I thought it might be a nice touch to leave the lamps on in their bedroom. I quickly flipped on the lamp by Daddy's side of the bed. It gave a nice, soft warmth to the room. I then walked around the foot of their bed to Momma's side and, reaching under the cream-colored linen shade, I felt for the small, round turn switch. One click, two clicks—nothing. I checked to see if it was plugged in and tried again, but Momma's lamp wouldn't turn on.

"Daddy! Is Momma's lamp broken?" I called out, wondering if it had been broken for some time.

Daddy appeared quickly in the doorway. "What? No, it works." Perhaps doubting my ability to turn the lamp on properly, he came over and repeated the same motions I had. "It's broke!" he said in shock as he sat down on the bed, just staring at the lamp.

I went to check Momma's supply closet. It was organized in her trademark way—by seasons and celebrations. Hoping to find a lightbulb, I wasn't sure what area to check first. As my hands picked up streamers and balloons, my heart felt sick, breaking a little more with each precious memory I encountered. The "Happy Birthday" banner that she always decorated with, no matter who was having a birthday, was just lying there. I sadly realized she'd never be putting it up again.

"Did you find a lightbulb?" Daddy called out.

"No, still looking."

As I glanced at the top shelves, I saw the baby blue ice-cream maker with rock salt sitting beside it in a Ziploc bag. My mind flashed back to images of our old kitchen with this ice-cream maker sitting in the sink, making Big Red ice cream. That was our family favorite, made with delicious Big Red soda, Eagle Brand sweetened condensed milk, and lots of love. I remember the sound of the motor running, competing with the noise of our window AC unit in the background, both working to keep us cool on those hot summer days.

I looked to the right side of the closet—lightbulbs!

"I found some!"

After Daddy unscrewed the old bulb, we both noticed nothing seemed to be wrong with it. I suggested we try the bulb in another lamp, just to see if it worked. It did. The bulb shined bright.

I put a brand-new bulb in Momma's lamp, but nothing. No light. The lamp appeared to be broken from the source, from the inside.

"Momma's light is gone. She's no longer here, Daddy."

In this moment we both felt the reality that she was really gone.

I'm sure Daddy thought of all the Bible verses that mentioned light. We were mesmerized by this broken lamp. A lamp that would never light up again. Momma was gone, broken, and her light had left this room, this place. Just like the bulb we took and tried in another lamp, she had left a light in each of us, but we would need some time before it could shine again.

I know she was trying to tell us she was on her way out. She was still in the space in-between, as I like to call it. I imagined her hovering over us, gently covering us, just like she would cover us with a quilt on a cold winter night. She was staying close, making sure we knew she was okay, but if I knew Momma, she wanted to make sure *we* were going to be okay. I could hear her whispering to me, "I'm so sorry this happened. I am so sorry. I didn't want to leave you."

Momma was always there, no matter when, no matter where. She was a constant in my life—a faithful, unwavering presence. I can remember only one time during my entire childhood when she wasn't present. I was in second grade, and my parents had gone out of town unexpectedly for two nights. I stayed with my Meme, my dad's mother, who lived across the road from our house. I missed Momma so much, and I'll never forget the feeling of joy when they returned, me running to her and her running to me. To this day, I recall the exact spot in Meme's yard where this happened, and I can still see Momma kneeling down to look at me, on my level. "I never wanted to leave you, Thelizabeth," she said. "I'm so glad to be back here with you." That memory holds one of the warmest hugs I've ever felt in my life. Her arms enveloped me, and I was tucked deep inside her love.

Back in her bedroom the morning of her funeral, I felt like I was experiencing something that was outside of this world. It was beyond where Daddy and I sat on the bed. It was a presence that we felt but couldn't interact with. It was Momma. She was letting us know that she had left this earth and, like a mama bird prepares her babies to leave the nest, she was preparing us for what was to come—a life on earth without her, without her light. It would no longer be shining from her side, but it would live on in us. Soon we would bury her in the ground, and all that would be left were our memories and the spirit that was hers. We understood that she was telling us she was leaving, but we would be okay because we had each other.

Not recognizing it at the time, I now see that the food and the lamp were both signs from Heaven showing me a path I didn't know I could travel. Not only did I need to feed on the comfort of food from friends, but I also needed to feed on God's Word and what He had in store for me. The light that Momma had always cast so brightly was now a light that I could shine. I guess you could say she passed me her torch.

Because I was so fogged up with grief, everything was too blurry to allow me to see it for what it was. But just a few weeks later, I would begin to connect the dots on the mysterious things that were happening in my life—things I knew were from God.

The rawness of grief is not something that people want to talk about. In fact, they do the opposite. This is true with many things that are uncomfortable. We hear about the stages of grief, but what about the stages of *healing* in grief? We won't ever totally "get over it," but we *will* get through it. How? By committing to our healing.

The word *commit* is defined as "pledging to a certain course." How could I commit to anything when grief had seeped in and poisoned every part of my existence? Throughout this book, I want you to remember the word *commit*. Let it bring you back. Each time you begin to stray away from the healing path, think, *commit*. God is right there, committed to you. He just wants you to commit to Him—and to yourself.

Facing reality in a world without our loved ones is beyond difficult, but we can begin to step into a place of healing. We can commit to finding hope. That is how we keep moving forward.

And just remember, it's not as scary as it may feel—especially when the person you lost is there with you, showing you the way.

Think Points

- During the most raw and vulnerable times after your loss, did events happen that forced you to face reality, like my accident with the ATV and the plow?

- Did you see any signs after your loss, such as a flickering light or a lamp going out, that you thought was a sign from the individual you lost? What were those signs?

What is one way you can *commit* to your healing process?

....

....

....

....

....

....

....

....

....

2

Scrambled

When emotions stir,
just remember where you once were.
—Theo Boyd

THERE WERE ONLY THE two of us in my parents' house that morning in August 2019. My daughter had headed back to college for a few days, my husband had returned to work, and my sister had gone back home to make sure she had suits ready for her boys to wear to the funeral services. So that left Daddy and me in the house, alone for the first time without Momma.

The house was quiet, except for my dog, Manly, who was trying his best to play with Barney, Daddy's dog. They liked to run around together outside, and I knew Manly was helping Barney cope with the loss of his main caretaker. We had pulled the pair of blue jeans and the blouse Momma had most recently worn out of the dirty clothes hamper to put in Barney's dog bed, hoping to give him a bit of comfort. We were all trying to comfort one another, and Daddy and I both welcomed the relief—and distraction—our dogs gave us those first days.

It's hard to say when the tears stopped flowing that week, since they never really did. Daddy's powder-blue eyes had completely changed into soft, sorrow-filled pools, brimming with a weight too heavy to hold. The power behind his pain slowly etched itself into his face, deepening the color around his eyes, pulling his shoulders forward as if grief itself had settled into his bones. Every movement was a little slower than the one before, and his words mostly disappeared, but I could tell thoughts were still running through his mind, as if he were searching for something lost that he would never find again.

I knew he liked a good fried egg, nothing fancy, but I needed to pour myself into something, so I made Daddy a hearty breakfast. I grabbed a whisk and beat those eggs senseless. I added some milk, cheese, salt, and pepper and poured the mixture on top of the butter that I had melted in the skillet. My mind was beginning to drift off with memories of Momma as I looked at her red rectangular "Butter Makes Everything Better" sign hanging right above the oven range. My daughter had picked that out for her just a few years earlier, a reminder of their not-so-secret shared love for butter. I could have stood there staring at that sign for hours. It was like my mind was on its own time—grief time. I needed to set a timer on my memories, something to bring me back to the present moment.

"Thank you for cooking breakfast for me, honey. I don't always eat scrambled eggs, but yours taste just like Sue's," Daddy said, interrupting my thoughts, and I realized then how much I had missed his voice. His voice had changed in the few short days since the accident.

Daddy had always had a strong voice, a voice that let you know exactly what was happening or needed to happen. When he spoke, you listened. But the voice I once knew had disappeared, just like Momma. He wasn't the same. Nothing was.

"Let's take these boys on a walk," he said with authority, motioning to the dogs.

Walking wasn't something Daddy ever suggested. Momma would always want him to go on walks with her and Barney, but he usually didn't. He preferred to sit on the couch watching *Law & Order* or documentaries with titles like *How Salt Shaped Society.*

"Let's go. A walk sounds like a good idea, Daddy," I responded, attempting to put on my shoes and brush my hair with only one good arm to use—and not my dominant one.

"Yeah, y'all go on, and I'll catch up on the four-wheeler," he blurted out as he went out the back door.

"What? That's not a walk," I said as the door shut. "Well, boys, I guess it's just us."

We had a big day ahead of us. The funeral home was supposed to be calling sometime in the morning to let us know when we could see Momma. I was so anxious to be with her, to be near her. This day held so many heavy emotions, all of them stirring fast inside me.

As I walked down the gravel road, I realized that Daddy had already taken off on his four-wheeler. I tried to follow the engine sound, but the sounds of birds singing and dogs playing were making that difficult. At first, I thought he was headed to feed the fish in one of the nearby ponds, but it was getting harder and harder to hear the motor, and it sounded like he was getting farther away. *What are you doing, Daddy? Where are you going?* I didn't need anything else to worry about, and now I had more anxiety to add to my already shaken self.

"C'mon, boys, let's go," I said as I started to jog toward the old farmhouse. I was supposed to be taking it easy, following the doctor's orders. But I had to make sure Daddy was okay. He was in a severe state of shock and sadness. Grief hadn't even had time to creep in yet.

I finally realized where he was going. Bold and brazen, there it stood. The tractor that had started everything, that had taken everything. And there was Daddy standing next to it.

"Daddy, what are you doing?"

"I just needed to see with my own eyes," he said as he leaned on the four-wheeler, looking up at the driver's seat.

"See what? *See what?!*"

Daddy started walking around the tractor, investigating, but I wasn't having it. He could do this another time. I had questions myself, but now wasn't the time. I felt like throwing up, but I hadn't been eating, so there was nothing in my stomach. My head was pounding, my heart was racing, and I just started screaming. It was probably a much-needed outlet, but at the time I actually scared myself. I didn't know what was happening, but I let the hurt and pain out with an awful sound.

I stayed right behind Daddy as he continued to look up at the tractor seat from all angles. He seemed to ignore my screams; he was unreachable in that moment, lost in his own sorrow. We were two broken hearts, neither of us able to put the pieces back together, neither of us able to understand the reason why this terrible tragedy had happened.

"Get on that damn four-wheeler and go home, NOW!" I screamed.

"No, I'm just going to get up there and look at something," he said with a glazed look in his eyes.

"No, you're not! You're going home. I don't want to be here!" My voice had reverted to that of a child. "Daddy, please, please! Come home with me. We aren't safe here."

Uncertainty had taken over my brain and body. I was so worried that Daddy was going to hurt himself. I grabbed his arm with my one good arm, crying and screaming. I pounded on his chest. "Please, Daddy, please, please, come home. Momma is gone. Momma's dead. We can't figure anything out here. I hate it here."

He looked down at me, wiping away my tears while his were falling just as fast. Then he hugged me. "I'm so sorry. I'm so sorry. I'm so sorry. Let's go back, honey."

Without saying anything, I climbed on the back of the four-wheeler, and Daddy drove us home, the dogs following behind.

I will never forget that morning, although I have tried. I keep it in a place I rarely visit. I was scared of everything I saw and heard that day. Daddy wasn't himself. Neither was I. His voice had changed, and it wasn't the voice I knew. I needed the Daddy who always knew what to do. I needed the Daddy who shared his wisdom at just the right moment. I know now that he needed to understand what had happened during the accident just days before, in the instant that forever ended the earthly connection to the love of his life.

I share this story to show how complicated grief can be, especially immediately after a tragedy. The two of us had a shared grief—both of our worlds completely scrambled, just like the eggs I had made Daddy for breakfast. But we also had our own separate pain and needs, and we each had to go on our own journey toward hope and healing in the years to come.

The Farmer's Tear

Morning, noon, evening, night,
Not a field out of sight.
Watching, waiting, wishing,
Plowing, planting, pushing.

Looking to Heaven, praying a prayer,
Paying the price, hard to bear.
Cultivating crops and counting cattle,
A monotonous, mundane battle.

Rippling hum from a tractor's start,
Piercing memories straight through the heart.
Tragic, true, fierce, forever weathered,
A bond unbreakable—shattered, severed.

What once made him whole,
Is now soil on his soul.
Forgotten prayers, abandoned, buried,
Love remains, burdens carried.

Dirt disturbed, planters in place,
Separate season, giving grace.
Resting reminder of fleeting years,
The legacy of the farmer's tear.

Theo Boyd
Father's Day 2023

Early on in my grief, everything was mixed up, cooking and sizzling inside me, blending in ways I couldn't understand. I didn't know how to process any of it. My emotions were overflowing, spilling out everywhere. I didn't know what my grief was going to turn into or how to turn it into something good. I struggled to share it with others. But as I took time to heal, to allow counselors to help me, to let others in and learn from my experience, I started to taste the fullness of it all. I started to experience hope.

But just like life has highs and lows, grief and healing processes have moments of relapse. *Relapse* is defined as "a deterioration in someone's state of health after a temporary improvement." You go through the low and reach the high, only to be dropped back down again. The smallest things can spark a memory that leaves you scrambling, sad, crying, and distraught. And you don't know what may be lurking around the corner that might make you fall back into despair.

I've experienced moments of relapse many times over the past six years. The feelings I thought I had dealt with were still present, making me vulnerable. I hadn't realized they would continue to affect me in the way they did. I can hear a sound, smell a certain scent, or hear of a family going through loss, and *BAM!* Relapse. Yes, grief rears its ugly head. It never leaves us, and it can show up, sneak in, hit hard, and pull us back to where we started from, and when we least expect it. We move forward, only to be brought back to a moment when we still had the person we lost. It's as strong a feeling as the sadness can be.

My best advice for when relapse hits you is to recognize it for what it is, embrace it, and keep moving forward. You are strong. Repeat these words: "I am strong." Don't let despair take you back down the road you just came from. Embrace grief for whose it is—yours. And if you don't feel like you can be strong in this moment, lean on a trusted friend.

Life is a concoction of going up, down, sideways, backward, and upside down. It's a scrambled mix. We hear something that reminds us of a specific day or brings us back to that traumatic time in our life, and we immediately feel like shutting down. The trick to being able to straighten out this scrambled mess is to be aware of the words that can bring us back to center each time.

I was a scrambled mess in the months that followed my mom's death. I knew I wasn't right. I knew I was off. I knew I needed to lean on those around me, and I did. Those women, who were there for me throughout all the losses and times of deep sorrow, whom I call my fairy blonde-mothers, showed up in my life, time and time again. They magically appeared when I needed them the most.

Throughout the grief, and in other difficult moments to come—including getting divorced, learning to run the farm, taking care of my land, and living my life thereafter—I couldn't have done it without them. My fairy blonde-mothers were sent from Heaven, and so was my counselor, Gale. She had the words that would bring me back to myself. One of the most consistent people I've ever met, she helped me move forward. Her wisdom continues to pour into my life as I recall every precious moment I spent in her office, up until the day she suddenly left this earth.

God was overseeing all these people—how they would impact my life and when they would show up. He was also holding me in His hand the entire time. He put people in my life who gave me the gift of being present. Whether it was to let me rest, let me cry, let me eat, or just let me grieve. They were there for me. *Present.*

There is no mistaking the tricks that grief will play on your mind. For days and weeks, and sometimes even now, I find myself reaching for my phone to text Momma. I continued to look for her in the kitchen. She had disappeared from the world, *my* world. Deep down, I knew what the facts were, but I couldn't fight the feeling of wanting to create an alternate reality. This is what happens when you are suffering from traumatic loss. A part of your brain is in protection mode, slowly revealing the truth, bit by bit, while another part is biting off chunks at a time.

> *Grief is a normal protective process. This process is an evolutionary adaptation to promote survival in the face of emotional trauma.*[2]
>
> —Lisa M. Shulman, MD, American Brain Foundation

As a child, I had an uncommon ability to handle certain situations better than most. I wasn't impervious to trauma or suffering, but I grew up with a strong sense of self. That's why when my mind started playing tricks on me, I knew something wasn't right.

Self-awareness is defined as the ability to recognize and understand your own thoughts, feelings, and behaviors. I had developed a strong foundation for self-awareness as a child, but it also takes time, education through counseling, and, as the days pass, the commitment to continue living a life *worth* living.

76% of grieving Americans believe that a better understanding of their emotions before a trauma or tragedy would have helped them cope better.

I always wanted Momma to be proud of me, and this didn't change even after her physical body left us. If anything, my desire to make her proud became stronger. *How would she want me to be there for Daddy? How would she handle this situation if it had been me who had been run over by that tractor?* I was working hard to rationalize my thoughts so that my feelings would follow suit. "Just breathe; it'll all work out," I could hear her saying to me in her soft, sweet voice. And every time I heard her words, I savored them.

The tractor left the farm in February 2023, more than three years after the accident. It was taken by a nearby farmer who wanted to restore it. I had no desire to ever hear that tractor run again. I was thankful someone wanted to take it away, to lift that burden from my family and me. To remove a painful sight we had to see every time we turned down the road and headed for the driveway. I had asked many people throughout the years to help me "get rid of that damn tractor," but it seemed like everyone I asked was hesitant to do so because of all the emotions attached to that old piece of red steel. That tractor was a physical, painful reminder of what we had lost, and its presence was a memory we had to keep reliving each time we looked at it.

It was a Sunday afternoon, cold and windy, when the tractor took its final trip away from the farm. It felt good to blame this piece of steel for all the wrongs that had happened. It felt good seeing it leave the farm, gone forever.

I heard from the man who restored the tractor that he'd finally got it running again. I didn't care to know anything about it, but God knew I needed to know the truth. He put the right person in the right place at the right time, so that I would hear confirmation that the brakes and clutch had to be replaced. They didn't work at all. When I learned this, I sat motionless and started to cry. Daddy had been so worried that he had made a mistake, that his wife's death had been his fault. But he hadn't made a mistake; he had simply started a machine that was broken.

"Oh, how I wish Daddy were here, so I could tell him it was *all* the tractor, nothing that he did or didn't do," I said as I looked at the man with tears in my eyes.

My mother's death had been a horrible accident, but my dad had blamed himself every second of every day, until the end. He couldn't live with the blame that lived inside him.

"He knows now," the new owner so sweetly reminded me.

Yes, Daddy knows the truth of *all things* now.

As you work through your grief and try to find some hope and healing, you'll have all kinds of reactions and emotions. I like to use *SCRAMBLED* as an acronym for healing. These are the action words that have helped me in my journey of self-awareness and healing. I didn't know them until I started to apply them in my life, and looking back, I realize I was *scrambled*—but in a positive way. You could say I put the cart before the horse, so to speak. When you're living with grief, and you find yourself searching for the meaning and purpose in your life, you will feel scrambled quite often. Use that word to help empower you in your healing journey to live the life you were put on earth to live. Whenever it feels like you're all scrambled up inside, remember these words of advice.

Scrambled

S is for *Serious.* We must take our grief seriously. "Hasn't it been a few years?" "Your parents would want you to be happy." "Are you still doing that grief thing?" These were just a few of the comments I heard when my mood was not as chipper as some felt it should be. Learn to feel comfortable enough in your grief to be able to speak up when this happens to you. Come up with a crafted and carefully measured response for when comments take you back or when your guard is down. I like to respond with two words: "That's interesting." Unfortunately, with grief, we often have our guard up. Take your current feelings, emotions, and your gut seriously.

C is for *Commit.* Commit to yourself, commit to healing, commit to your future. Each day, I make the conscious decision to focus on what I want and need to get done in that day. I realize that with grief, some days it's hard to even get out of bed, but as the days and weeks go by, if you are able, start committing to do something that will help someone else. It's in that space where you will find fulfillment and meaningful reasons for living. Helping others has been one of my greatest joys in this journey, and I am *committed* to it.

R is for *Ready*. Are you ready to move forward? I wasn't, and the more that people told me when or how I should be doing something, the more I pushed back against them. Just as a teenager rebels against a parent, I rebelled against what everyone else thought I should be doing. I heard "advice" such as: "You shouldn't dwell on your grief." "Maybe you shouldn't write about grief so much." "I don't think anyone will want to read a book with the word *grief* in the title." Did I listen to them? No. Some of those words would circle in my mind as I pushed forward, but I kept on the path that I felt strongest in, knowing that God had taken care of me for this long, and He would know when I was ready for the next move in my life. In my book *My Grief Is Not Like Yours*, I titled a chapter "More 'F' Words" where I explain the importance of getting more Faith, Family, Friends, Fun, and Food in our lives. My faith, my friends, my foundation—all of these "F-words" helped me get *ready* for the road I was about to travel. And I have loved every part of this road, potholes and all.

A is for *Acceptance*. This is probably the hardest thing to do. Accepting a situation that is not comfortable and not what we wanted is beyond difficult; it's maddening. But I have learned that acceptance is where peace comes from. I didn't want

Momma to be dead, or Daddy, or my counselor Gale. I didn't want my husband to leave either. I didn't want to be alone, but there I was. And as soon as I started to accept where I was and what was happening, I could take the first step toward healing. In order to grow, we must accept where we are, even if it's not in a place we want to be.

M is for *Mindfulness.* The mindfulness it takes to be aware of where we are socially, mentally, and emotionally as we grieve takes strength, a combination of faith and grit that comes from deep inside us. In order to be present in each moment, I started practicing yoga. This is an activity that you can't fake. You're either all in, breathing deeply and hoping not to fall while in tree pose, or your mind wanders and you tip over. If you don't want to do yoga, try some breathing exercises. Breathing reminds us that we are here, living. When you're mindful of your physical self, you're automatically in tune with your emotional health. And before you know it, you are socially alive again.

B is for *Boundaries.* Oh boy! There's that word everyone loves to use when they are trying to get something they want. Boundaries are needed, and they're great—*if* they are helpful and healthy. But be careful that you aren't putting up such strong boundaries that you keep out the people and interactions needed to heal and move forward. Boundaries can be a slippery slope in grief. If you can't make the recipes your mom always made, don't. If you don't feel like going out to the dinner you were invited to, it's okay. But don't set up rigid boundaries for anything and everything. You don't want to live in isolation or fall into the cracks and crevices of grief. Be aware of your boundaries and keep them healthy. If you feel someone is not respecting you, that is usually a sign that your boundaries are not clear. Focus on yourself and your own needs before focusing on what others are doing wrong.

L is for *Learn.* We never stop learning, and that is true even in periods of grief. I have learned so many things I never wanted to learn, so many things as grief became part of my life. One of the most important things I have learned is that there are more people grieving than meets the eye. Some people hide their grief because they don't feel they can openly express their feelings in a society that tends to brush grief off to the side. Grief is an opportunity to learn. It may not feel that way, but with each stage of your journey, you are learning something about yourself. If you are a caregiver, you are learning what your limits are, and if you are the one being cared for, you are learning how to let go and surrender yourself. I learned how to live without the people I had depended on the most for advice, support, and love. I learned about me. I learned to lean on God and my faith for the next move. I started to pray again, and I had the thoughtful prayers of friends. One day, I was lying on the shower floor, trying to figure out how I would get up, how I would keep going. Then, before I knew it, I was standing tall again. Learning about *what* you are experiencing and *why* is the key to living a healthy life with grief as your new companion.

E is for *Expect*. As you grieve, very few people will really understand what you are going through. I wish the world would have treated me as delicately as a China doll in my grief, fearing that even the slightest movement would break me. Unfortunately, that didn't happen. Society *expects* us to get over things quickly and return to who we once were. So expect this to happen, learn from it, and don't let it hurt you. Instead, let it strengthen you and push you forward so you can eventually help others. Momma always said, "If you think about what other people might be going through, you will act differently." In your interactions with other grievers, give them grace. Because of what you have been through, you can advocate for other broken hearts. Give yourself grace along the way too.

D **is for *Decide.*** We all have decisions to make about our lives. In grief, you often feel like all the decisions have been made for you. You're left without the one you lost, maybe left alone, maybe without the one you depended on most—your love, your life. It's hard to move forward, but we all have decisions to make about how we are going to do that. I decided I was going to live a life that would make proud those I had lost, in any way I could. I'm still working on that every day, but I love that I get to decide.

If you have trouble remembering what *SCRAMBLED* means and how it can help your grief journey as you find hope all along the way, here is a way to remember it:

> I had to be *serious* and *commit* to be *ready* and to *accept* the present, while staying *mindful* of my *boundaries*; if I wanted to *learn* and *expect* more from others and myself, I had to *decide* how I was going to move forward.

What once had been a daily trip to the cemetery after Momma died turned into a weekly trip as time passed. After Daddy died, I started going back more consistently, visiting them both. I enjoy my visits to the cemetery. Its location is only a one-minute detour from the main highway that I travel frequently. Once inside the cemetery, you hear the soft sounds of cars passing in the distance, which creates a white noise that is both peaceful and pure. Not to mention, cemeteries make great dog parks.

Manly roams around within the fenced perimeter, while I make my way to where Momma and Daddy are. I'm not naïve in believing their spirits are limited to that space, but it gives me a landing place to feel, talk, and be with them—and only them. The distractions of life are hushed. All I hear is the crunch of leaves under Manly's paws as he tracks the scent of a squirrel down and around the trunks of trees. Many years ago, Daddy and Momma bought a concrete bench that sits within the Boyd family section. It's a great resting spot, allowing me to catch them up on the latest happenings as I watch Manly scurry about.

I treasure the time I get to spend there, time for reflection, time that seems to stand still. I am able to be alone in my thoughts, but I'm not really alone, of course.

On one particular visit, having been in town most of the day running errands, I decided to stop by the cemetery on my way home. Aside from the usual talk about how my daughter, Reagen, was doing in law school, or what Manly and I were up to, this time I asked for a sign.

Hey, Momma and Daddy, can you send me a sign? I really would like to get a sign from you. I miss you both so very much, and I miss the feeling of having you here with me. I miss the sound of your voices.

I sat there, watching the sun fading away to get ready for another day. When no obvious sign appeared to be coming, I got up to leave.

"Manly, come on! Let's go. Let's go home." These words usually serve as a sign for my dog to run in the opposite direction, hoping I'll chase him. "Manly, come on!" Hearing my serious tone, he did his usual snail walk back to me. He finally made it to the car, hoisting his front body into the back seat while I lifted his hind end into the car.

Once we were loaded in, I started the car. As I grabbed my seat belt to buckle myself in, I noticed the display screen wasn't turning on. I'd never had a problem with it before. *Maybe it's a computer glitch.* I pushed the button to turn the car off and then restarted it. Still no screen. Then I touched the screen delicately, just as I would touch the screen of my iPhone to brighten it. It came on!

Well, that was weird.

I tried to adjust the temperature and turn on the radio, but the display was stuck on the call screen. Suddenly, I looked up to see the screen change and begin to populate with . . . voicemails? *What? What is this?*

At first, it looked as if the numbers were scrambled, but then I saw a pattern. A log with hundreds of voicemails was loading with dates going back as far as 2016. I hadn't been able to find voicemails in my phone for at least two years! And here were *hundreds.* I sat there motionless; I could barely breathe. I recognized the repeated number immediately:

254-582-9307

This was my parents' landline number since before I was born. I had just asked for a sign, and here it was. I began to shake nervously, as if I had just heard some earth-shattering news. It was a moment I will always remember exactly where I was, the time of day, and what the scene looked like. They call that a *flashbulb memory*. It will never leave me, and I will never forget it.

I wrote a poem about my parents' phone number and read it at Daddy's funeral:

582-9307

Through the years of my life,
In times of joy or strife—
I always had him to call,
And let my burdens fall.

As early as I can remember,
Be it spring, summer, fall, or winter—
I always had him to call,
And let my burdens fall.

You see, Momma couldn't hear me,
Daddy would listen and then she would see.
I always had him to call,
And let my burdens fall.

This farmer's daughter and preacher's too,
What I needed, he always knew.

I always had him to call,
And let my burdens fall.

From a little girl to who I am now,
We talked about God, Jesus, weather, and cows.
I always had him to call,
And let my burdens fall.

The number remains,
But the location changed.
582-9307
Now he isn't there—he is in Heaven.

I always had him to call,
And let my burdens fall.

Theo Boyd
June 25, 2022

After Momma died, I didn't look for voicemails because everything I had from Momma was on text. Due to her hearing loss, she wouldn't call me; she would only text. As I described in *My Grief Is Not Like Yours*: "At eighteen months old, my mother became sick with a very high fever that lasted for several days, and as a result, she lost her hearing. The doctor did all he could, but the fever bore its weight in her ears, forever taking away one of her five senses."[3]

I probably read our old text messages every day for the first year she was gone. It was healing for me to relive our conversations about everything from farm stuff to daughter stuff and especially the endless recipe sharing. But Daddy always called, never texted. "I can't work a cell phone," he would say. After Momma was gone, I bought him a cell phone. I chose the one with the biggest buttons, one that would be easy for him to navigate. I sat with him on the bed and showed him how to work it. He tried so hard, but our lesson ended with Daddy throwing the phone across the bedroom, only to have it crash into a pile of old farm magazines that were serving as a platform for the small clock radio he loved to stare at. "I hate technology," he would say. I actually find myself repeating those three words often, thinking of him. Bless his heart, he really did try.

After Daddy died, I tried to find any voicemails from him that I could, but they were all gone. Nothing. In fact, I didn't have any voicemails from anyone. I even went to several different cell phone stores to ask them to help me. Eventually, I realized the voicemails that Daddy had left me just disappeared for some weird reason. I began thinking I must have deleted them and just didn't remember, kind of like when I was in the ninth grade and recorded Duran Duran songs over Daddy's cassette tape recording of his bedtime story, "Tom Turkey." Boy, do I regret that. Well, this was another one of those audio regrets.

Sitting in my Jeep that day at the cemetery, I reluctantly touched the first voicemail to play, adjusted the volume, and soon heard the voice I had been longing to hear for so long.

254-582-9307 . . . 6/6/17 00:24
"Aw, hello, hope y'all are doing okay. It's just startin' another day, went to see about the cows, shelling a few peas, not too many. We're sitting on the back porch. Hope you have a good day, hope everything is okay. Bye-bye, we love y'all."

254-582-9307 . . . 10/4/17 00:26
"My name is Joe Bob Boyd, my wife's name is Sue. We just hope you have a good day today, Thelizabeth. We love you. Everything's okay. We got a good rain yesterday and everything's okay. We're looking forward to today, we're having a great time. Hope y'all do too. Love you all, bye-bye."

254-582-9307 . . . 10/16/17
"Our name is Joe Bob and Sue Boyd, your mother and daddy. We love you and hope you have a good day. Take care and bye-bye for now."

Daddy was so funny, saying who he was, as if I could mistake that voice for anyone else. He would call, and if I didn't answer, he'd leave a voicemail every single time. If I missed a call, I knew I would soon have a voicemail to listen to. Momma was always there in the background, as she couldn't take part in a phone conversation because of her deafness. Daddy was our "translator," so to speak.

We could all take a lesson from that. How often do I call someone instead of texting them? And if I do call them, do I even let it ring long enough to leave a message? I can't remember the last time I left a voicemail on someone's phone.

You may be thinking that I didn't have the right setting clicked, or I hadn't set up my voicemail correctly. But after I lost access to my voicemails, I changed my phone number and even changed cell phone providers. I gave up any chance of ever hearing or seeing those voicemails again. I guess they came from somewhere in the cloud—or clouds, you could say.

I specifically asked Momma and Daddy out loud to send me a sign, and I told them that I missed their voices. I desperately needed to hear the sound that could bring me home once again. And for the first time in years, I had them with me. I asked for the sign of their voices, and I was blessed to receive them.

Daddy, technology worked this time! I can hear you with Momma in the background. I can hear you both!

Now I can listen to the sound of being home again, anytime I want.

Think Points

Have you felt *scrambled* in your grief? How do you recognize it, and what do you do to get unscrambled?

....

....

....

....

....

....

....

....

....

....

....

What has been the hardest part of your grief journey?

....

....

....

....

....

....

....

....

....

....

....

How self-aware are you? Describe how you manage your emotions.

Do you have old voicemails or recordings of your loved ones who have died? How do you feel when you listen to them?

3

Medium

You have to digest life. You have to chew it up and love it all through.[4]

—Paula McLain

I LOVE THE WORD *MEDIUM*. Anytime I'm not sure about how to order my steak, *medium* seems to always hit the spot. I don't want it too dry, and I don't like it to be undercooked, but I do love some pinkish red in it. It's moist and easier to chew this way—full of flavor, sometimes even melting in your mouth.

Daddy would completely disagree. He was always a "well-done" type of guy. He used to say, "I've seen where those cows have been and what they eat. I want my meat cooked all the way." Regardless of how you order your steak—rare, medium, or well-done—sometimes the best things in life happen somewhere in the middle, in the medium area. And after the initial raw experience of loss and the scrambled, messy emotions that follow, much of grief is lived in the middle, between the extremes.

For many years, I had a counselor I adored. Her name was Gale, and I would talk with her about life's little struggles. But in 2019, she became my lifeline, keeping me above water when I was drowning in grief. She had such a beautiful way of creating visuals with her hands to explain feelings and emotions and how to work through them.

My favorite visual was when she would explain that we don't gain ground when we are extreme in our focus. She would hold her hand flat and horizontally as she moved it up above her head and then slowly lowered it all the way toward her feet, explaining that "nothing good happens here or here . . ." Then she would raise it back up, right in front of her face, right in the middle: "But right here. This is where it is. This is where we learn the most."

Gale would tell me how life is full of extreme highs and lows, but it's the middle that really matters.

In grief, it seems like our only options are the highs and the lows. We forget what it's like in the middle, on the medium side of life. When we find that sweet spot, the place that feels like home for us, we can get a better handle on healing. It's hard to tell someone who is experiencing an extreme emotional high or low that they should talk to a counselor, and it's even harder for that person to hear. When we are "in it," we don't want to hear anything, even if deep down we know it will help us. We must give space for the grief to settle.

> 68% of grieving Americans say if they knew how to get help for dealing with their grief, they would.

Daddy used to say, "You can't witness to someone who's starving. You need to help them and feed them, make sure they're safe. Once you minister to them with compassion and bring them out of that dark place, then you can start talking about the light and our hope in Jesus."

Daddy would often write poems for funerals that he officiated, especially for people he knew well. But if he was speaking at the funeral of someone he didn't know well, he would read a poem by Linda Ellis called "The Dash." The poem's title refers to the dash between the two dates on a person's tombstone, and words of the poem ask us to examine how we spend our lives in the dash time, how we make the middle years count. After he read the poem, Daddy would often ask, "How's your dash going?" Even though someone had just died, and their dash had just ended, he wanted the mourners to take note of their time left, to give serious thought to how they were spending their lives.

The Dash[5]

I read of a man who stood to speak
at the funeral of a friend.
He referred to the dates on the tombstone
from the beginning . . . to the end.

He noted that first came the date of the birth
and spoke the following date with tears,
but he said what mattered most of all
was the dash between the years.

I find it sad that the two dates on a person's tombstone or in their obituary are their birth and death dates. What about that middle? Didn't it matter? I don't know about you, but I almost start hyperventilating, worried that one day others won't know what I did in my dash.

With a commitment to healing, a desire to live each day to make the people I love proud, I live with hope. I get to be a testimony of God's love for all to see. That's a great place to be in this life, living with hope. It's a beautiful spot in the middle. It's the medium.

If we let life's low points get to us, they will consume us. There were many times, early in my grief, when I didn't feel like getting out of bed, or I didn't know if I even could. At those times, I thought of Gale's words reminding me that there is always another day: "Try the next day."

The same goes for food. At the height of my sorrow, I wasn't eating because I had no appetite, but when I learned that food is nourishment that helps our body heal, I started to eat again.

Grief can knock us down. We can either let ourselves be devoured by it or get back up and show up for life. Momma was an example of this. She was completely deaf, and for the first ten years of her life, she couldn't communicate beyond body language and hand gestures. She had to climb so many mountains throughout her life. But she never took life too seriously, and if she relapsed or was at a low point, I never knew it.

77% of grieving Americans say not being able to talk openly about grief has created a grief crisis in our country.

Over the past several years, I have experienced some of life's harshest blows. In that time, I've discovered that grief can't be forced down or ignored. It must be worked through, like kneading a tough dough until it's pliable. I've seen what happens when we shove it aside, ignoring it, thinking we'll get to it later, only to have it rise up at the worst moment in the worst way.

Those who take time to work through the process, explore their feelings, and allow room for release and growth have a healthier outlook on the future. Their ability to recover and learn to live successfully with grief is night and day from those who beat it down, hoping it will just go away. The out-of-sight, out-of-mind mentality doesn't work with grief.

With the help of a counselor trained in your specific type of loss or grief, you can gain the tools needed to help yourself move forward. Your knowledge and awareness will grow, and eventually you will feel well equipped to handle life with your new constant companion, grief. You'll be like a fully furnished kitchen, with every appliance, utensil, and cooking tool you could ever need.

I first started visiting Gale's office in 2002, long before Momma and Daddy passed away. At that time, I had a blended family, a booming career, and a busted sense of self. I didn't have boundaries or even know what those were. I needed objective advice from someone who didn't know me. Friends and family will offer plenty of unsolicited advice, and while it can be well-intentioned, it's almost always biased and not exactly what we need to hear in certain situations. Gale became the much-needed third-party voice in my life. And on the night of July 29, 2019, when I lost my mother, my relationship with her proved to be my saving grace. I needed to hear words that were going to help me in my immediate and dire state. Gale was there for me, and the toolbox she and I had been adding to over the years was there for me to pull from.

When Gale died suddenly in 2020, I grieved the loss of a woman I not only respected but also had grown to love.

With direction, encouragement, and compassion, she had helped me find the *me* that had been lost for so long.

I have had the privilege of seeing some very good counselors in my life, and now I have found another lady of wisdom who helps me move through life with a little more ease. Mary Ann reminds me so much of Gale, especially in the way she listens and takes whatever my problem of the week may be and helps me process it in a different way, with a new perspective. I miss the feeling from being in Gale's office—the comfort and clarity that only she could provide. I am thankful to have found another woman who listens with love, and I know Gale would approve.

Don't be afraid to visit several counselors. And know that it may take you a while to find just the right fit. Continuing your counseling visits, especially when you face grief, is critical to healing. It's one of the most important decisions you will make, so take it seriously. If you don't seem to feel the right connection with someone, keep searching until you find the right "Gale" for you.

It had been a few weeks since my last therapy appointment, and life was super busy. My frenetic schedule included a book tour in Texas and numerous podcast, radio, and television interviews, not to mention regular trips to the doctor, dentist, and Manly's vet appointments. My calendar reminded me of a recipe with a dozen steps that I would probably never attempt. But there it was, showing me a list of challenges for the day, each one with varying degrees of difficulty. As overwhelming feelings started to rise up, I thought, *Take one bite at a time, one task at a time.*

Many of us struggle through each day, kidding ourselves that we are the only ones experiencing this busyness, and we rush to check off as many things as we can from a seemingly never-ending list. No matter what we try to do to alleviate the "extra" in our lives, it still finds us, and we are sent spinning like a top that never stops. In grief, those days are more common—the days of focusing on everything else until we get so busy we forget what really matters. When we finally come to a stop, that's when we see what it was all about. Maybe we needed the chaos of that day for the sign to come through more clearly.

On this particular day, which had been filled with errands, I got home later than usual. I was hungry, but I refused to eat until I had "washed the day away." I made it to my bathroom, started my shower so the steam could begin to relax me, and got my music going. One of my nightly rituals is listening to '80s soft rock, smooth jazz, or classical piano. I give Alexa my music request, and voila—I had music!

Once the piano music started playing, I showered and washed my hair while my mind played a carousel of the day's events. After the shower, I gave Alexa the command to turn off my music.

"Alexa, off."

I walked out of the bathroom, cradling my clothes. But the music was still playing.

"Alexa, off."

I came back in to give the command a third time, this time from a closer position. This had never happened before. She'd always understood my voice.

"Alexa, off!"

She wasn't turning off. At this point, Alexa had my complete attention. I dropped the clothes to grab my cell phone and began recording. This was a sign, and I wanted to prove what was happening, to others as well as to myself.

I had never heard the song that was playing before, and since Alexa had won our back-and-forth battle, I leaned in to listen. I couldn't place the melody, but the voice sounded familiar.

I tapped the record button on my cell, and with one more "Alexa, off!" I noticed something. Each time I tried to turn the music off, it got louder and louder:

May the peace in your heart give you joy in your heart.
May your heart know the meaning of love.
May the love you will know, when you know you're in love,
Be forever and ever as true as the love I have given to you . . .
That's my wish.

—Jimmy Durante, "My Wish"[6]

When the song finished, I gave one more "Alexa, off" command. The music completely stopped, and I stood there in shock. Then, replaying the video I had just taken, I sat in my makeup chair and soaked it all in. *Was it Daddy? Was it Momma?* I think it was both of them, together. They were letting me know that the day of demands and hectic hurriedness was inconsequential to the most powerful force on earth—love. Love overshadows it all. I didn't know it then, but soon there would be love coming my way.

I picked up my dirty clothes once again, turned off the bathroom light, and glanced back at Alexa. Her light was off, and there was no music. The sign had come and gone. I was thankful for the moment I'd had, for the words in the song, and for the reminder that love transcends time and space.

We can forget that God doesn't want us to be so stressed and busy that we miss opportunities to see Him and feel His love. He wants us to trust Him to take care of all the parts of our lives that take away our joy. He wants us to look to Him for answers. If we let the worries of today take us away from Him, they will. He wants us to talk to Him, to pray and feel heard in ways that we don't here on earth. He wants us to know that He loves us and that He has the answers we are desperately seeking. This sign, this song, reminded me that I was loved—that I didn't need to sweat the small stuff.

You are here, and your life is meaningful, and someone may be missing out if you let yourself get caught up in the chaos of the day. Remember, love is all around you. You are living out your dash in every moment. Through all the falls and failures, stay focused on your path, the one God intended for you. Lean into the signs that surround you. They will show you your way, and they'll help make your dash full of love, full of memories, as full as God intended your life to be. Keep your eyes focused on God, and He will help you fill that dash with meaningful moments.

Think Points

- [ ] If your life were a steak, how would you want it cooked—raw or medium, maybe burnt? How do you see your grief?

....
....
....
....
....
....
....
....
....
....

- [ ] Have you had any signs appear when you were distracted, overwhelmed, or busy? Maybe through music or technology?

....
....
....
....
....
....
....
....
....
....

How do you think that counseling or a lack of it has affected your grief and healing?

....

....

....

....

....

....

....

....

....

....

4

Sunny-Side Up

For his anger endureth but a moment; in his favour is life:
weeping may endure for a night, but
joy cometh in the morning.
—Psalm 30:5 (KJV)

Time had stopped. Momma had died, and with her death went all sense of time. I didn't know what time it was or even what *day* it was. I was lost, caught between the before and after with no awareness of past, present, or future. It was all so foggy, but even in that dark moment, there were glimpses of light. Just like a lighthouse guides a ship to shore, when light emerges, you can't take your eyes off it. Hope is there to bring you in.

The morning after the horrible accident and Momma's death, I vaguely remember visitors coming in and out of Daddy's house, bringing food or just giving Daddy a hug. One of our visitors was my cousin David, Daddy's nephew. He would preach at both my mom's and dad's funeral services. David brought his wife, Connie, with him to comfort our family, just as Daddy had done with Momma hundreds of times when tragedy struck someone he knew. Now, Daddy was on the other end of it.

"But joy comes in the morning," Connie said, as she walked in from the garage to see Daddy for the first time without Momma.

I remember this moment so clearly. With tears streaming down her face, Connie had come to bring some peace to us. I've never forgotten her words or where she was when she said them. *How could any joy come this morning?* I'd wondered at the time. Looking back, though, the sun came up that morning, and I was there with Daddy, and the light was shining on us. Since that day, each morning I wake up and think, *But joy comes in the morning.*

From the moment my first book was released, I have experienced more joy than I thought possible. Joy amidst pain. The sunny side of life is focusing on the light and looking up—sunny-side up. If all we do is look down at our watches, our phones, and our agendas—or even look down too much at our own grief—we miss what God wants for us: bright and sunny days filled with hope. Put down the noise, and sometimes even the pain, and you'll be delighted by how much lighter and sunnier you feel.

In late 2019, after Momma died and Daddy started to decline, both emotionally and physically, I struggled to come to terms with the fact that my life would never be the same. Accepting that, and being able to adjust to a new life, a life without her, was *the* hardest thing I have ever had to do. I poured myself into my writing, my passion for others who grieve, and my deep desire to bring something new to the table of grief.

Writing a book isn't easy, but selling books is also hard, especially when you aren't famous. I don't care about fame (although I've never turned down an open mic), but I *am* dedicated to giving grief a voice and changing the face of what grief looks like in our culture. It's what I was put on earth to do.

Some people never find the meaning in their life, and they struggle to discover their purpose. *Meaning* is the thing you are most passionate about, and *purpose* is using that passion to help others. Even knowing that our meaning and purpose will change as our lives do, I have never been so certain of what mine were until I began writing down my intimate thoughts and feelings about grief. Until I was able to put my pain on the page, I never truly knew fulfillment. Sharing my writing with others who grieve and meeting those who have connected to my words have meant so much to me. It's the fuel I need to keep going forward. It's the closest thing to teaching and seeing that look in children's eyes when they finally understand the concept you are explaining. The past six years have been filled with those aha moments.

80% of grieving Americans believe that having a purpose in life helps them heal from their most recent grief, tragedy, or loss.

With most things I set out to do, I do them *all the way.* That includes writing books. My desire in *all* my writing is that someone will read something that speaks to them, realize they are not alone, and understand that hope is there waiting for them. Mark Twain said, "The two most important days of your life are the day you were born and the day you find out why."[7] I know I was born to write *My Grief Is Not Like Yours.* That book was like my baby, and I have treated it as such. As I watch its audience grow, I am so very proud of its message and how it's helping broken hearts.

However, no one told me that marketing the book would be the difficult part. With every bookstore I visited for book signings, I saw the competition from floor to ceiling, wall to wall, bookend to bookend. What could I do to make my book stand out, to bring my story to life, so that those suffering in silence could read my words? I needed to think outside the typical bookselling walls.

After some careful consideration, I called an old friend.

Ron and I had met in the fall of 2019 at the Dallas Cattle Baron's Ball, where I'd recognized him immediately. "You're Ron Corning from Channel 8!"

"Yes," he replied. "And you are . . . ?"

We talked for quite a while and even exchanged numbers. Ron was a very popular news anchor for WFAA-TV Channel 8 Dallas/Fort Worth. His face was familiar and his smile contagious. Something told me then that I would need his advice, guidance, and expertise in my book journey. God has a way of placing people in your path you will need, so it wasn't too long after our initial meeting that I reached out to Ron. We have remained friends since the day we met, sharing a mutual understanding of grief, books, media, and just about everything. His calm way of preparing me for interviews gave me the confidence to speak with more clarity and helped my message reach more people who needed to hear it.

By the time my book was released, I hadn't talked to Ron in a few months, but when I eventually did, we picked right back up with each other as if no time had passed. And it wouldn't be long after this quick catch-up phone call that we would meet out at my family's farm and bring the book to life.

"That's a wrap!"

I had never been so happy to hear those three words in my life. I had planned the events of this day with Ron and his media crew from Dallas and Kristi and Shan, the two amazing women who work with me. We were filming the book trailer for *My Grief Is Not Like Yours*. As I continued to learn the book business, I discovered that trailers are not just for movies—they're also used to market books.

We picked a February day. We didn't know at the time we scheduled it that the weather would be cold, with temperatures in the low forties. It wasn't raining—the sun was actually shining brightly—but the wind was so strong that it cut right through the cotton farm dress I was wearing and even the jeans I'd put on underneath. During the interview, I was shivering so hard my teeth were chattering.

We filmed everything at the farmhouse where I'd grown up—and where the accident had happened in 2019. It was important to capture the beauty of my childhood home, and to do this, we decided to record most of the dialogue inside the house, where there was no electricity, which also meant no heat. The crew brought in lamps and generators, but nothing could give us the warmth we needed. So we just powered through the day.

We arrived at the farm around nine o'clock that morning, bags full of hair product, makeup, and a variety of dresses to choose from. The day was full of takes and retakes, filming anything we thought could be used for the trailer. We were fitting all the footage and dialogue into one day, due to my limited budget. I remember Daddy always said he loved the low-budget films the best. Well, he would have loved this one, because my budget was about as low as the temperatures felt that day. (A few weeks later, I was shocked that you couldn't see my teeth chattering in the finished product.)

As soon as we got situated, I noticed the two camera guys walking around and filming family knickknacks, our old piano, and various pictures and decorations still hanging on the walls. In 2013, my parents had moved into their new farmhouse across the road. No one had lived in the old farmhouse from my childhood for ten years, but it was still filled with memories. It was interesting to watch the photographers as they took pictures of things that Momma would have said "we probably need to throw away." Some of the smallest items would appear later in the film crew's video collections from that day, such as the little ceramic cross with the word *Faith* written across the top that Momma had hanging above her kitchen stove.

When Daddy and Momma moved, they took bits and pieces of their lives with them, leaving behind most of the old furniture and household items. Momma wanted new furniture in the new house, not having purchased any new pieces since she and Daddy had gotten married. She had planned on removing all the items from the old house eventually, but time has a way of pushing us forward, and for Momma, going back to the old house was moving in the opposite direction than she was accustomed to. Daddy consistently mentioned the old house with a quiver in his voice; I know he missed it so much. I did too, but we were both overjoyed that Momma had finally gotten the new home she'd longed for and deserved. They were both very thankful that the new house had a central AC and heating unit, windows that opened and closed without the help of a crowbar or a block of wood to keep them open, a roof that never leaked, and toilets that always flushed without a plunger or coat hanger to assist.

As the camera crew moved from one room to the next, I stayed in the living room, preparing for my interview with Ron.

Working to adjust my microphone so that my jewelry didn't interfere, I noticed the camera guys making their way back into the kitchen. I looked up to see Ron taking the clock down from the wall above the sink. This was a battery-operated clock that had been hanging on the wall since my parents had moved out in 2013.

"I want to adjust it to reflect the time you mentioned in your book," he explained.

In *My Grief Is Not Like Yours,* I recalled the night Daddy had died and the visions and feelings I'd had of being right there in that house, the house I'd grown up in:

> *How was this feeling coming to me? I questioned it, but I didn't fight it. I smiled, feeling all the love again. I smiled,*

seeing Daddy at his rolltop desk studying, seeing Momma in the kitchen putting the meringue on one of her chocolate pies, and me, soaking it all up and hoping that they knew I was there . . .

He was home again.

I opened my eyes and looked at the clock on my nightstand. It was 12:30 a.m.[8]

"What time was it? I don't have the book with me," Ron said.

I will never forget that time as long as I live: "12:30," I quickly replied.

Ron looked up at me with disbelief. "That's the time it was set to."

The room got quiet. Looking at one another, we were all silent for what felt like several minutes.

"That's been happening with things all over the place!" Shan blurted out. "This is another sign, Theo. We have to write this down."

"Yes, that's the time, 12:30. That's the time in my book. That's the time Daddy died."

Although the death certificate stated the time I had called 911, which was 8:39 a.m., the funeral home staff and sheriff's office all told me it had been approximately eight hours between the time Daddy died and when I had found him.

Daddy did everything with meaning, with purpose. I knew he'd chosen Father's Day and the time of his birthday, 12:19 a.m., to end his life here on earth. The time 12:30 would only be eleven minutes later, and it made sense to me that this was when he'd taken his final living breath.

"You promise you didn't already adjust those hands to that time?" I asked, already knowing he hadn't.

"No, I promise, Theo. I hadn't adjusted it yet," Ron replied.

One of the camera crew added, "I have a picture of it from earlier. I already photographed that clock."

The room was so quiet and cold, as we all waited to see if the clock really was set on 12:30 the moment we entered the house.

"Here, here it is."

We all moved in closer to see the picture on his camera's little window.

The old kitchen clock that I hadn't paid much attention to through the years now had *all* my attention. It had stayed behind after my parents' move, hanging in its same spot above the sink. The sun was peeking through the window now, casting a small ray of light across its face. I felt validated in my gut but had this looming doubt still hovering over me. It's one thing to have a feeling about something, but it's entirely another when you see it in real time. *Real time.* I saw the time that I had been sure was right. This was confirmation that my vision from that night, the night of June 19 at 12:30 a.m., was real. Daddy had come to me that night to let me know he was home again. He was back in our old house, the one that held all the memories.

That clock is one of my favorite signs because of its seeming insignificance. It was just an old clock hanging on the wall of an old farmhouse, left behind, but now it will never be forgotten. That clock is going in the house I'm now building on the farm.

As the day progressed, we all laughed, cried, and worked hard to get what the crew needed to make a spectacular book trailer. We put in a full day's work, and we all knew Momma and Daddy were in the farmhouse with us on that very cold, sunny day. We were all there together, back home. It was a sunny-side up kind of day.

Think Points

Have you had any signs or feelings that your loved one who passed away is right there with you? Have you ever experienced a sign with a time or a date connected to it?

....

....

....

....

....

....

....

....

....

If you could set your clock to any specific time and day, what would it be? Why?

Even in a dark time, have you experienced a sunny-side-up moment—like a Bible verse, a note from a friend, a light guiding you, or a person from your past who showed up at just the right moment?

....

....

....

....

....

....

....

....

....

5

Over Easy

Be willing to feel the flame that will fill your heart.
—Theo Boyd

I HAVE BEEN MARRIED THREE times. I still find it hard to believe, but it's the truth. When I was a little girl, I would dream of the day that I would wear Momma's wedding dress (although I don't think I could have fit into it) and marry the man of my dreams. Sometimes, she would let me wear her veil and pretend I was getting married, and the man I would marry would be Daddy. *Don't all little girls with amazing fathers wish for that?*

With each marriage, I did my best to make it work, but sometimes life doesn't go the way you planned or had hoped for. When I see couples who have been together since high school, I always wonder why I never found that one true love who would last a lifetime.

It was just another Friday night in the fall of 2022, but I'd decided to go to the local high school football game to watch my hometown Wildcats play against a longtime rival. I hadn't planned on going to the game, but when I drove past the field that day, I thought of how much my parents had enjoyed the games, plus I knew I needed to start getting out more. I had loved watching the drill team perform and remembering how it felt to march out on the field at halftime, praying I'd remember all the moves. My favorite part of those nights was the third quarter, when all the band and drill team members had permission to leave our section to visit family and friends in the stands, and eat those unforgettable nachos that only taste good when you're eating them in the bleachers. Yes, I needed some Friday night lights to help distract me from my grief and loneliness.

I sent a quick text to a couple of childhood girlfriends who lived close by to see if they wanted to join me, and Wendy and Crystal agreed to meet me there. It had been a few months since I'd seen them at Daddy's funeral, so we had a lot to catch up on. We reminisced while eating our concession-stand nachos in the bleachers. As we talked about old times, we laughed, and I realized I hadn't done that in a while.

"How are you *really* doing?" Crystal asked.

"I'm good. I'm really doing good." The conversation quickly turned to my love life, or lack thereof. "I don't want to date or get in a relationship right now," I explained.

"Why not?" they asked.

"I've been through this all so many times that I just don't want to do it again. I'm tired."

As the conversation continued, I did admit that going out to dinner or a movie with someone might be nice.

"I miss the affection and touch of another hand on mine. I miss the feel of arms around me," I said softly.

We all giggled like little girls. We were talking about boys again, just like we'd done so much during our teenage years. I felt my face getting warm and blushing a little.

"Okay, that's enough about that. Let's watch the game," I said in my teacher voice.

My friends let me off the hook, but not without a quick selfie to commemorate the moment. Wendy positioned her phone to take our picture, while I rushed to wipe the cheese from my bottom lip. "Smile, y'all!"

After Wendy took the picture, she kept typing on her phone—with a soft smile but also a slightly deceitful look in her eye, like she was planning to rob a bank after the game.

"Who are you texting?" I asked.

"Oh, just a friend. A friend you should go out with."

"What? No!"

"Okay, you don't have to. But he's really sweet . . . and he's a farmer," Wendy added, as if that little revelation might change my tune.

"Uh, no way. Momma and Daddy would be so upset. They wouldn't want me to date a farmer," I said as we all laughed.

As a matter of fact, another girlfriend, Carol, had mentioned a farmer to me just a few weeks earlier while we were in an exercise class together. I had told her no thanks as well. But now I was starting to wonder, *Is this the same guy?*

Farming is a very hard and stressful line of work. Daddy joked often about how Momma really lucked out getting to be a farmer's wife *and* a preacher's wife. Growing up, I witnessed the difficulties and stresses of this lifestyle. Farmers wear many hats, or caps, for that matter. It's not just planting seeds, watering, and watching. Farmers are agronomists, economists, meteorologists, plumbers, welders, engineers, electricians, general mechanics, and chemists—any role that is needed to be a steward of the land. It's stressful to depend on things that are far beyond your control. And a farmer's wife has to be able to roll with it all, which was not something I wanted or needed right then.

The night reminded me of when Daddy and Momma would go to a football game to have a little date night. In the early 1960s, Daddy had been #88 on the Whitney Wildcats, playing wide receiver. He always said he could have played so much better if he'd had better shoes. My grandparents didn't have much money, but in those days that was common. Daddy laughed when he told me how my Meme, his mom, took him to the five-and-dime in town to get him a jockstrap and a pair of cleats. The cleats had holes in two places and were high-topped, so he had a hard time running in them, and he swore the jockstrap had been used before. Daddy was six four and as skinny as a T-post. Even at a young age, he learned to accommodate what he was given with what he needed.

Momma had been a high school cheerleader in Itasca, a small town about thirty minutes north of Whitney. I'm sure she enjoyed going to the football games with Daddy on date nights, imagining herself back on the sidelines, feeling the excitement under the Friday night lights. There they were, the football player and his cheerleader, sitting beside each other and cheering each other on for almost fifty years. I could feel them there with me on that night, as I watched the game with old friends.

Deep down, I knew Daddy and Momma would probably love the idea of me going to dinner with a farmer. We would have so much in common and so much to share. I could talk about Daddy's crops and cattle and what it was like growing up on a peanut farm. Maybe socializing with someone who shared this lifestyle and knew where I was coming from would help ease my grief. After all, I had been wanting a companion, someone to go to dinner or watch a movie with. I could share Daddy's funny jokes or maybe some of Momma's recipes, if he liked food. And maybe it would help me to not feel so lonely anymore.

But no, I wasn't ready for that quite yet.

"Don't give him my number, please," I told Wendy. "Just don't." I was adamant.

I had hardened to the fact that heartache and hope could coexist. I felt guilty when I was happy. I knew this was just grief trying to consume me, but it was something I consciously fought. I didn't think happiness or good times were something I would ever experience again. And because I'd had trouble with relationships in my past, I thought I didn't deserve another chance. Three strikes, you're out! That's what I told myself about love.

87% of grieving men and 53% of grieving women think choosing to love again is necessary to move on with their lives after experiencing loss.

Even though I was trying to help others find hope in my writing, I was struggling to apply the words to my own life. I could tell my readers how to learn to live with grief, to move forward with hope, but I wasn't allowing myself the space to do so. But we must practice what we preach. Grief had become an all-consuming part of me—wholly, fully—pulling me into that dark space that I warn grievers about. I needed something to snap me out of this place.

"What are you laughing at?" Crystal asked Wendy as she giggled while looking at her phone screen and typing feverishly.

"Wendy, what?!" I asked, also wanting to know what was so funny.

"Okay, he's texting me that he had a date a few weeks ago that didn't go so well. He's asking if you're allergic to peanuts."

"Well, I hope not. Daddy was a peanut farmer," I quickly replied, wondering if they had talked about me before.

My curiosity had gotten the better of me, though, so I asked her about this mystery man she couldn't stop texting. She proceeded to explain that a girl he had dated recently was allergic to peanuts, but because he was unaware, an innocent kiss goodnight had sent her to the hospital.

"Gosh! That's awful," I replied, still thinking about how peanuts had played such a big role in my life.

Wendy continued to text with the farmer as I watched the game. Part of me hoped this opportunity would pass me by, but another part of me hoped it wouldn't. After the game, we all went home, and I didn't think any more about this farmer or the peanut kiss.

It was Labor Day weekend. My fairy-blonde mothers were scheduled to come down on Friday and spend the weekend with me, but they'd had to delay the trip by a day. It was just one day, but when you're alone, one day can feel like a month of Sundays.

That night would be another one spent alone, with just my dog, Manly. He's a great companion, but I think even he was getting tired of our one-on-one consultations. His smirky facial expressions were like, *Lady, get a grip and get a life*. He was right—I needed to get a grip and get a life. I just didn't really want to.

The hardest part of doing anything that is good for us is getting over that initial hump, the jump into something unknown, uncomfortable, and uncharted. It's like taking that first step onto the treadmill or rolling out a yoga mat. We dread it, but it ends up being the best thing we could have done for ourselves, and we come out on the other side so much better for it. It's like making a recipe we've never tried before, scared it won't turn out right. Then one day, we have an extra burst of energy and we go for it, and whether it works or not, we prove to ourselves we can do challenging things. But we'll never know unless we try.

I didn't want to be alone one more night. I *can* be alone. I enjoy my me time, but my gut was telling me it was okay to talk to someone who was open to talking to me. Momma always said, "If you feel it deep down, it's right." I was feeling like this was a sign that it would be okay to talk to this stranger, and since I was alone for the evening, I decided to just go for it.

I texted Wendy and told her she could give the farmer my number. It had only been twenty-four hours since she'd been texting with him at the game, and now here I was saying, "Call me!" How desperate was that?

What am I so afraid of? I just wanted to have someone to have dinner with occasionally or maybe to go see a movie with. *Where is this fear coming from?*

I was young when I married my first husband. He had been my high school sweetheart, but we really had no business getting married at such a young age. I was nineteen when I walked down the aisle for the first time. It was a beautiful church wedding. Daddy performed the ceremony, and Momma was my matron of honor. But the marriage didn't last long, less than five years. We were too young. I thought I'd known what I wanted. I'd gone in with my whole heart, but that romance quickly faded, and I was left with only pieces that had never had a chance because the foundation wasn't strong enough.

My second marriage happened too quickly after my first one ended. I was living in the big city, still pretty far from home, lost and searching hard to be found. I was fresh from the farm, trying to find my way and doing it all alone. In my mid-twenties, I was scared and didn't want to be seen as a failure, so I quickly rebounded into a blind date that ended up being an eleven-year marriage. This marriage led to my life's most beautiful blessing, my little girl. I will always be grateful for that. But as the marriage fell apart, despite me working hard to hold it together, I realized that some things are out of our control.

My second husband and I both tried to make it work, but on my daughter's ninth birthday, we separated. Not ideal, I know. She loves to remind me of this—how I ruined her birthday. I've spent years explaining to her how I didn't want it to go down like it did, and now it's just a funny little stab from her every now and then. We usually laugh about it, but I know it was difficult for her. It was difficult for all of us.

In those times when we feel our hearts breaking, we can wonder what God has planned for us. Heck, sometimes we even wonder if there *is* a God. We might find ourselves on a road we shouldn't be on, but we didn't pay attention to the warning signs, so now we're left stranded, stuck, and standing in the ditch. How did we get here? And how the heck are we going to get where He intends for us to be?

But God is always there. *Always.*

My motto when I graduated from Whitney High School was Proverbs 3:5–6: "Trust in the LORD with all thine heart; and lean not unto thine own understanding. In all thy ways acknowledge him, and he shall direct thy paths" (KJV).

Deciding on my motto had been a struggle, and I remember asking Daddy about it. He'd never liked his own motto—"Live life as it comes"—and wished he'd picked Proverbs 3:5–6 instead. That's all I needed to hear. After reading those two verses and knowing Daddy would have chosen them, I knew that was the motto for me.

He shall direct thy paths. God is there to guide us, encourage us, and direct us to the life He has planned for us, but we sometimes go our own direction. I should have leaned into the Lord with my heart and let him direct me, but I still thought I could figure it out myself.

They say the third time's a charm—or maybe a charmer. I intentionally did not allow myself to even think of marriage again. I knew I didn't need a man to help me. I had a daughter, and she was my number one. But, like everything else in life, things happen when you're busy making other plans. I fell again. Too hard and too fast.

Once again, no one measured up to Daddy and the standard he'd set. My third marriage ended after twelve years, and it shared some characteristics with the other two failed attempts but at a greater level. This marriage lasted longer than the other two, and the separation and divorce just about crushed me. It happened during my darkest days. It knocked me to the ground, but through all the tears, I was able to rise up. My tears were like the rain, falling to help a seed find its way up through the soil. Although I didn't realize it at the time, there was a seed of strength buried deep in my heart.

That's what I'm here to share with you—the beauty we can find inside ourselves that will allow us to bloom again. God sends the tears to help us heal, just like he sends the rain for living things to grow. Pretty soon, we find our way, we sprout, and we grow up through the dirt. We must be patient, like the farmer, waiting to see if what has been planted will have the strength to grow, filling the fields with fullness and beauty, a bounty of hope.

Lost in my thoughts, I felt my phone buzz with a text.

> This is Ronnie Joe. Just saying hello.

Oh my gosh. A text. From a man!

My heart began to beat fast, I started pacing back and forth, and I told Manly I didn't know about this. He just gave me that stare that I'd become accustomed to. I didn't respond to the text right away. I just let it sit.

After some time, another text came through.

> Feel free to respond. I'm just looking for a friend.

I continued to let it sit.

I made a promise to myself that I would do things differently from now on with men. No more quick moves to satisfy a temporary feeling of loneliness. And with the tragedy and trauma I had been through so recently, I needed to move slowly and think cautiously in order to protect my fragile heart.

Apparently, I was moving *too* slowly for Ronnie Joe. Another text came through, just six minutes later.

> I'm going to bed. Goodnight.

I guess he didn't think I would be responding to him.

It made me smile and laugh a little, so I decided to write back.

Ha ha ha
Hello, this is Theo.
I'm actually looking for a friend too.
I'm headed to bed myself.

Even though he didn't give me much time to respond, I was happy to hear from him. I was eager to talk with someone, and I didn't want to miss out on a potential date for dinner or a movie. Most of all, I didn't want to miss out on the possibility of making a new friend. I didn't realize it at the time, but I was about to see hope in a unique yet familiar way.

Ronnie Joe texted back, and we got to know one another a bit through our messages, laughing out loud and discussing everything from farming to food to friends to furry companions and everything in between.

How do you like your eggs?

Over easy.

No way! Me too!

This seemed to be a big deal to Ronnie Joe. He even discussed it several more times with me. He'd never dated a girl who liked their eggs the same way he did.

We continued texting that night for over an hour, both holding back on just calling each other to talk. Texting was easier, safer. I was nervous, and I like to think he was too.

Everyone calls me Theo.
Except my Daddy.
He called me Thelizabeth.

You can call me Ronnie Joe.
My father is Ronnie.

Ronnie Joe. Oh my goodness, these Southern name combinations make my heart so happy. My Daddy was Joe Bob, and this man was Ronnie Joe. Both having *Joe* as a part of their name was one of my first hints this was a sign from above, not to mention Ronnie Joe also being a farmer. I knew this sign was from Daddy. It had only been two months since Daddy left this earth, and he didn't want me to be alone, so he sent a farmer my way. Of course he did! This was a sign I couldn't try to reason away. It was like Daddy was saying, "I am here for you."

Sometimes, the signs have to be that way, don't they? We can be so quick to try and make sense of things when we should just be open and accept what is. What are the chances there would be a single man, with kids the same age as my daughter, who was also a farmer and living near me?

After hours of texting, I finally received a very specific question:

Can I call you?

Oh yes, good! My fingers are sore, LOL.

I could feel there was something more this farmer wanted me to know. When the phone rang, I picked it up immediately.

"Oh, hello. It's good to put a voice with the name," he said.

"Yes, how are you?"

For almost three hours, we talked about everything from the farm, family, and friends to cattle, crops, and cooking. As we were about to bring an end to our first conversation, he said he needed to share something with me.

"I'm deaf."

Not sure I'd heard him correctly, I asked, "What? What do you mean? You're hearing me just fine."

"I wear two very expensive hearing aids, but without them I can't hear you. I lost my hearing when I was seven years old from a cholesteatoma."

I just sat speechless, holding the phone to my ear, but with no words to say. He proceeded to explain how it had all happened—the illnesses, the numerous doctor visits, and the doctor who had practically performed a miracle saving him.

Does he know about Momma? How could he? Maybe Wendy, Crystal, or Carol told him? I had to know if he knew.

"Okay. Did you know my mother was deaf?"

"No, I didn't."

The reality of this didn't sink in until the next day when I was thinking about how Momma had lost her hearing at a very young age. My thoughts began to swirl. *Daddy was a farmer. Momma was deaf. I lost them both, but now I've found someone who might be able to fill a void in my life—a very real void. Have I found a companion—maybe a love, maybe the sense of belonging I've always dreamed of?*

I had thought it was a sign from Daddy, sending a farmer my way, but was Momma in on this too? A farmer *and* someone who had lost their hearing—two of the most indicative traits of my parents combined in one person. *WHAT?*

I reminded myself that Daddy never did anything without Momma, and Momma never did anything without Daddy. Yep, they both had a hand in this. But the biggest hand was God's. He gave us free will and will let us do our own thing, but He will never stop working in our lives to direct us, and even sometimes chasten us. I will admit God has had to do more than His fair share of that with me.

I often hear from women thanking me for admitting to my three failed marriages. They were embarrassed to admit to theirs, but when they hear me openly sharing, they know they are not alone, and they shouldn't be ashamed of any part of their journey. It's in the journey that God reveals the key to what He has in store for us. We want life to be the way *we* want it, tempted to keep ordering our usuals or going for the quick and easy fare, but God may have an unexpected treat in store for us. He may be cooking up a new menu item, and we'll be so glad we tried it. Whatever we order, His hand is always guiding and nudging us along.

My story is still being written. I'm still finding my happily ever after. It's in the hand that I hold, the arms that wrap around me, and the hope that fills my heart. I was given a sign from above. I guess I'll never really know if it was Momma, Daddy, God, or all three of them, but I do know I'm thankful for my over easy love.

And he calls me *Thelizabeth*.

Think Points

If you have lost a love in your life, what do you miss the most about them?

....

....

....

....

....

....

....

....

....

....

....

Do you have a new love? Describe what you love most about them.

....

....

....

....

....

....

....

....

....

....

....

How do you like *your* eggs? Do your eggs describe you or your relationship in any way?

....

....

....

....

....

....

....

....

....

....

....

6

Rare

It was so wonderful to be there, safe at home,
sheltered from the winds and the cold.
Laura thought that this
must be a little bit like Heaven,
where the weary are at rest.
—Laura Ingalls Wilder, *The Long Winter*[9]

This morning, I was supposed to wake up to snow. Well, at least that's what my weather app told me. I felt the same excitement as I did when I was a child. I ran over to the window, flipped on the back porch light—but no snow. I quickly turned on the local weather channel, hoping that maybe, just maybe, there was a chance I would see snow today.

In Texas, snow is not something we get to experience very often. It's rare. Instead, what we usually have the privilege of dealing with is sleet, ice, slush, and mush. When snow does fall, it does so like cars passing through my hometown—if you blink, you might miss it. The snow turns the usually dull Texas landscape into a glistening Thomas Kinkade painting, a dusting of white covering the ground like a blanket reflecting a soft glow of light.

Today, I just had a feeling snow was coming my way. I was hopeful because of the memories that come with snow, even though they can cut me in two. Those memories involve Momma and Daddy—my childhood, the farm, the precious memories. My heart ached with homesickness, the longing to be right back there in those moments. In grief, a good memory can be rare, and sometimes I wonder if even our good memories can be a detriment to healing. It hurts to remember how things once were, knowing that the future looks different, and that reality can be frightening.

Learning *how* to remember while moving forward is part of my life now. I move forward, but I bring my loved ones with me in everything I do. My memories are mine, but I've found that by sharing them, I can help others. And myself. Sharing is cathartic. It shows us that we are not alone in facing things.

As I closed my eyes and recalled a memory with snow, I longed to be back there, back in that place where everything was soft and safe. I work to create new memories now, but I still acknowledge my past by continuing to tell the stories of my childhood.

Snow Days

Is it going to snow? I remember going to sleep while Daddy watched the news, listening intently to the weather. It was rare in our neck of the woods, but every few years, we would get blanketed in white.

I remember waking up and running to my parents' bedroom. Being just tall enough to peek over the windowsill, I would stand on my tippy toes to see outside. Momma would be there watching for my reaction, with Mrs. Baird's bread bags in hand. Daddy was already out feeding cows and checking fences.

Momma would bundle me up in my coat, scarf, hat, and mittens, while carefully placing small pieces of cotton in each of my ears. Bending down, she helped me step into the bread bags that she had been saving for the occasion. Tightening them around my calves, she tied each of them in a knot to keep my feet dry, and I was off!

Opening the front door, I got my first whiff of the cleanest, coldest, most breathtaking landscape that was snow—*our* snow. I inhaled so deeply that the bitter cold burned my throat. My first steps onto the white carpet were crunchy, and I reached down to touch the covered ground, feeling the cold seeping through the threads onto my hands. I buried my face in my mittens to smell and taste the beautiful, white, cold powder. Momma would scoop some up in a small bowl to make snow ice cream for us later.

I hear the tractor. Daddy would soon be coming in from feeding the cows. He would jump off and chase me in the snow, pretending to be a snow monster. Momma would laugh and take pictures.

I still hear the laughter.

I still feel the love.

Daddy built a snowman, while I watched, hoping to learn. Momma brought a carrot for his nose and a broom for him to hold, and Daddy found an old hat to top him off. We had our snowman!

Over the next few days, we watched the snowman slowly leave us, and I began praying for another snow to come.

As I stated earlier, where I'm from, we usually just get the yucky part of cold weather in Texas. We also suffer extreme heat, icy winter days, skunks, snakes, scorpions, and infestations of bugs that only make Texas their home. And chiggers. If you are from the South, you know about chiggers! They are microscopic mites that live in hot and humid areas. If you go out walking in tall grass, they will find a home under your skin, and the itch they cause is horrendous. You don't know aggravation until you experience a chigger bite.

All these conditions and characteristics of my part of Texas make those of us who live here a little stronger. At least, I like to think so. They are all part of what made Momma, Daddy, and me resilient, ready, and a little more rugged than most. Sure, I dream of living in a picturesque cabin like the kind you see on Instagram or Pinterest, one where there are no bugs or hot temperatures. Where the snow softly falls outside my window as my dog and cat lie beside each other on my plush feather bed, while a cup of caramel coffee sits steaming from the crisp air. The kind of scene where you can feel your body relax and ease into the experience of living there, putting your feet up to warm them by the crackling fire.

Like snow in Texas, or a good memory when you're grieving, falling in love is also rare. Sometimes, rare things come as a surprise. Is it that we're not open to seeing the love God is providing for us, or have we stopped looking because our heart has been broken too many times? The key to love is understanding that it is always within our heart, broken or not. Love is a beautiful gift from above, but we must make the choice to let it out or let it in. The heart is always ready to heal you with love.

Last year, we didn't have a white Christmas. There was no snow on the ground, but it was still chilly outside. Ronnie Joe took me out for what would be our first Christmas date. We had been dating for about four months by this time, and we decided that before our kids came home from college and the chaos of the season set in, we would exchange our gifts and celebrate *our* Christmas with a special dinner date. It would be a dedicated time for just the two of us.

I wore a black dress with my blue "Carrie Bradshaw" Manolo Blahnik pumps. These were the shoes I had worn on our first date, and I loved that I had an occasion to wear them again. In my grief, I have found that retail therapy can often be as helpful as a good counseling session. The joy these shoes have brought me far outweighs the guilt I sometimes feel over buying such a high-priced indulgence.

When I arrived at his house, Ronnie Joe was wearing a dressy pair of blue jeans, a starched shirt with pinstripes in soft fall shades, and a new pair of Red Wing boots that he said he was breaking in. Those boots were a familiar sight for my eyes. Daddy always wore Red Wings. Each Christmas, Momma would get him a new pair.

After dinner, we went back to Ronnie Joe's house to open our gifts. Because he hadn't given me any specific requests, I just went with a coffee mug, some kitchen items (because I knew how much he loved to cook), an ornament engraved with the date of our first Christmas, and a framed picture of us. We took turns opening our gifts, and I loved seeing his reaction to each one. For me, giving is so much better than receiving. Well, it was until this night!

I began cleaning up the ripped wrapping paper and bows, separating my gifts so I could load them into my car. Ronnie Joe had gotten me a Bissell carpet cleaner, which I desperately needed with my dog, several household items, cozy and comfy blankets, and some kitchen items that I know he'd made a mental note I was missing, when he was cooking in my kitchen. I laughed at this thoughtful gift—he knew my kitchen better than I did.

As I was straightening up the living room, I looked up to see Ronnie Joe coming toward me. "We're not done. I always give the last gift," he said.

"What? What is this?" I asked as he handed me a small, navy-blue gift bag with a thick ribbon for its handle and silver metallic tissue paper shining out the top. It looked expensive.

"I wanted you to have this," he said softly.

I removed the shiny paper and found a small box inside, which was the same color as the bag. As I reached in to pull out the box, I thought about how beautiful my life had become. The emptiness I had felt deep inside for so long was slowly filling up, one moment at a time. With a huge, childlike smile on my face, I lifted the lid to see a beautiful necklace with a rose gold, heart-shaped pendant covered in diamonds, daintily dangling from its delicate chain. It was perfect.

"I love it so much! Thank you, Ronnie Joe." I kissed him and thought to myself, *He picked this out for me. When he saw this necklace, he thought of me.*

"I'm glad you like it. You have my heart."

And he has mine.

A few weeks before Christmas, Ronnie Joe had asked me if there was anything special I wanted that year. "I don't know. I really haven't thought about it," I said. It had been a long time since someone had asked me what I wanted.

"Well, it would really help if you would give me something to go on. I have no idea what to get you."

There was something I *had* always longed for. It seemed to be the one thing I could never get—a gift that was genuinely and uniquely chosen for me by the man I loved. I wanted something given without my advice or input, without my daughter guiding the purchase. I didn't want to have to send a link. I wanted it to be a link he made on his own, his heart connecting to mine through a thoughtful gift.

"I would like a piece of jewelry, nothing expensive, but something you pick out. Each year at Christmas, Daddy always got Momma jewelry. I would like to wear something that you choose for me."

By the time we were exchanging our gifts that night, I had almost forgotten that I'd told him I wanted jewelry. Oh, how full my heart felt when he helped me fasten my new necklace. I held my hair up while he fastened the closure. It was beautiful. It's what his eyes could see on me, and it was special.

A few days later, I got Momma's jewelry box out to look for a pair of pearl earrings I wanted to wear for New Year's Eve. I had gone through her jewelry after she passed, searching for something I could wear for her funeral. Since that time, I hadn't spent any significant amount of time looking at her little treasures. I'd told myself I would look through it more carefully when I wasn't so busy.

I pulled the little compartments in and out, examining the small bags that had notes inside them. Momma was always so good about recording when and where she'd gotten something. She would put the jewelry in its own little bag with a note taped inside. I loved reading those tiny messages written in her beautiful handwriting.

Immediately, one item caught my eye. I gasped. Manly jumped up and started barking. "It's fine, Manly. It's okay." I started shaking. *What? It can't be. Is this right?*

Inside the bag was a necklace with a rose lying on top of a heart-shaped piece of wood. The flower was rose gold. The note Momma had written to put with it said,

Rose necklace
Joe Bob gave it to me for Christmas
1st Christmas present since we 1st got married.
12-25-70

I called Ronnie Joe immediately. "When I told you I wanted a piece of jewelry for Christmas, did I tell you what kind? Like, did I say necklace? Earrings? Bracelet?"

"No, you just said jewelry. Why?" he asked, sounding a little worried that he may have gotten me something I didn't like.

I explained to him what I had just found, and we both got silent. We were in shock. And then I started crying.

"You gave me a rose gold heart-shaped necklace for our first Christmas, and Daddy gave Momma a rose gold heart-shaped necklace for *their* first Christmas together. This is crazy!"

He completely agreed. We *knew* that Daddy and Momma were the reason we'd found each other. We both knew we were a match made in Heaven, literally. We saw it then, and we continue to see it in the signs around us.

In grief, we can often focus on the negative aspects of everything around us. It's normal to do so, but we must remind ourselves to see the signs of hope and gifts from Heaven. The beauty beyond the bugs, the scenic setting sun that tells us the day is almost done, the snow that rarely falls but fills us with hope when it does.

When we start to look for the signs, we realize that they aren't rare at all. They are right in front of us, waiting to be seen.

Well, would you look at that—I'm looking out my window, and guess what I see?

Little flurries of snow.

Think Points

Have you found that good memories are rare in your grief and healing? What is a good memory of your loved one that comes to mind?

Have you experienced a new love in your life since your loss? Have there been moments when your new love has connected with your loss in a way you couldn't explain?

What are some rare but special moments for you in your grief?

....

....

....

....

....

....

....

....

....

....

7

Burned

Just like every night has its dawn
Just like every cowboy sings his sad, sad song
Every rose has its thorn.
—Poison, "Every Rose Has Its Thorn"[10]

HESITANT TO MARRY A third time, I had still done it. I was in it for life, staying true to my vows, but as time passed, outside influences would wreak havoc inside my home. The grief just brought everything to the surface. Grief is a filter, a very strong one. Nothing can get through without being strained. I worked hard at keeping an impossible situation possible. Letting go, accepting, and surrendering to the inevitable was heartbreaking, yet liberating. I could move forward, like Momma said, knowing that I had tried everything I could to salvage the brokenness in our marriage.

Holding on to what you thought life was going to be and recognizing what it *is* has been one of my hardest life lessons, but as Momma always said, "That's just life. We have to keep moving forward."

Only a few days after Momma's funeral, I decided to have her wedding band soldered on to my wedding ring. I thought it would be a beautiful way to always carry her with me. Well, this union didn't last long. Soon after I did that, I learned of my then husband's infidelity, and I found myself back at the jewelry shop asking them to please take the rings apart. I guess I thought that putting Momma's band with mine would somehow magically help my struggling marriage. It didn't. Nothing could. I had gotten burned—badly burned.

"Just give us about a week," I heard the jeweler say. As I looked up, I could see he was looking at me with the saddest and most sorrowful of looks. Of course, it didn't help that I was crying the entire time.

Marriage never really worked for me. I have come to realize that it wasn't just the affairs, the deception, the distrust, the lies, the insecurities that ended my marriages. In every relationship I had ever been in, I had given everything completely and unconditionally—all of myself. I gave each of my husbands all they needed or wanted, neglecting an equally important thing—me.

I gave so much that I had nothing left for myself. I didn't know how to establish boundaries, or even what a boundary was, for that matter. With the example my parents had shown of what marriage should be, I lost sight of myself and my reality.

If something bothered me, I just ignored it or assumed I'd eventually fix it. The amount of time I spent calling girlfriends to get advice and go over issues I was having in a particular relationship would have been enough time for me to bake a hundred pies from scratch. (Just baking one pie from scratch takes me an entire day, from crust to meringue.)

You could say that I've been forced to find myself, and boy howdy—have I ever! Not only have I found myself, but now I love me! I even take myself out on dates. I enjoy going to the movies, going to restaurants, shopping, and sleeping in, all by myself. Well, I do allow Manly to sleep with me. He has his perfect spot at the foot of my bed, but he loves to gradually scoot up beside me, and I'm okay with that. He's a good source of heat when nights get cold.

It's taken me years to get to this place. After getting burned so many times, I had to work hard to get here. Now I'm in a place of curiosity, confidence, and comfort. It's the best feeling in the world! I can buy myself flowers, as Miley Cyrus sings. But I will say that nothing beats a beautiful bouquet bought for you by someone who really likes you.

It was our first date, and Ronnie Joe surprised me with a big, bright vase filled with a dozen red roses with white daisies sprinkled throughout, making it the most beautiful red and white bouquet I had ever seen.

"Oh my goodness! Did you know daisies are my favorite flowers?"

"I had no idea. I just thought they looked pretty with the roses," Ronnie Joe responded with a look of surprise. "The flower shop I always use was super busy, but they let me go back there and create this arrangement myself."

"Well, they're perfect! If this farming thing doesn't work out for you, and if you don't think you'll open a restaurant one day, you could always be a florist," I suggested.

Daddy had always loved arranging wildflowers for Momma. He always said he would have been a florist if he hadn't been a farmer. He would spend hours out in the fields choosing bold bunches of color to arrange for Momma. I love flowers and the joy they bring to all my senses as much as Daddy did.

And now these crimson-colored, long-stemmed beauties scattered with dainty, white daisies, arranged with love from my sweetheart, were making my heart so happy.

In learning to live on my own, I've had to take charge of *me*. Within one year, I inherited part of an estate that I helped build during my marriage, and not too long after that, I inherited our family farm. With the farm and all that it holds, I made the choice to stay in Texas and build my life here as a self-sufficient female who will eventually get this farm up and running again, with cattle, hay, my dog, and maybe a barn cat or two. Oh, and I can't forget Dallas the horse. He's thirty-two and living his best retirement life, thanks to Nellene, Daddy's sweet neighbor who still helps run everything on the farm. She was a godsend for Daddy in his last two years, and she continues to be such a blessing to me. She is like a second mom to me and all the animals on the farm.

Embracing the hot and humid Texas climate has been the hardest hurdle for me to jump. The heat and humidity in Texas are grueling. Daddy used to laugh and say, "I'm a *humid* being." He was always quick to craft funny one-liners and play with words. Perhaps he was trying to keep his mind off the many plagues this state has to offer. Unbearable heat, grass burrs, fire ants, kissing bugs, red wasps, yellow jackets, crickets, mosquitoes, chiggers, scorpions (or *stangin' lizards*, as Daddy would say), possums, skunks, and snakes—the worst kind of snakes: rattlesnakes, copperheads, cottonmouths, and coral snakes. All poisonous and deadly. *Aaaah!*

Every morning when I wake up, I pray that I don't see a snake. That's one plague I could live without. It doesn't help to ease my fears that Momma was bitten by a copperhead back in 2018. This particular type of snake lives mostly in wooded areas and seems to like where our farm is located. I recently had some old oak trees that had died cut down, and the workers told me they killed sixteen copperheads while they were cutting down those trees. *Sixteen!* I still cringe when I think about that.

Usually, snakes don't start coming out of hibernation and slithering around until later in March. One February day, Momma was raking up some leaves in the backyard, and she got down to use her hands for just a minute. She always was a hands-on type of worker. As she began pushing the leaves to one side under the base of the tree, she felt a swish. Not being able to hear, she told me later that she just felt something in the air change. "It was so quick!" she recalled. She looked down and saw two little dots on her left hand between her index finger and thumb.

She ran inside, told Daddy what had just happened, packed up a few things, and went out to the truck. Momma was always poised and prepared. As she sat there waiting, she wondered where Daddy was. Then she looked up to see him with a big garden hoe in hand.

"I'm not leaving until I kill that @#$%!" he yelled.

After Momma finally convinced him otherwise, they were off to the hospital, where she would spend three days and two nights receiving multiple bags of antivenom. I told Daddy he'd better watch out because Momma might just become a snake after all that treatment.

The next year in March, Momma was clearing leaves again, but this time she was using a rake, not her hands. And she had a garden hoe with her, just in case. She was shocked when she stumbled upon a snake—a copperhead, in fact—and that day, the snake met his fate. She got him!

She went to the house to get Daddy and asked him to take her picture with it. She was proud, and I don't blame her. Momma was tiny and petite, but you wouldn't know it by all the hard work she did on that farm. As he went to take the picture, Daddy noticed the snake was still alive, but quite injured. He never let her forget that. But who cares? Momma overcame her fear—and her enemy!

> 64% of Americans grieving from a divorce or breakup feel they ignored the red flags they saw early in the relationship.

We all get burned sometimes, but there are almost always warning signs to look out for. Just like the thorns on rose stems, or the snakes in the grass, we can be aware of the dangers of relationships if we are looking for them.

In speaking of things to watch out for, I want to share some relationship thorns and snakes that can attack you, more commonly referred to as red flags. At the end of this chapter, I want you to write down some possible ones that you may have experienced or be experiencing now. I would be remiss if I didn't caution you about some behaviors that are *not* okay. This will help you clarify and define them, and then you can ask yourself, *Why am I putting up with this?* Hopefully, you won't have anything to write in those lines, but if you do, it's better to get them out in the open rather than tucking them away to fester.

Relationship Red Flags

Crying on your birthday. Often when one party in a relationship feels they are not the focus, they will manipulate the situation, causing the other person to feel bad. In a twisted way, this makes *them* feel better. Recalling something you confided in your partner or a disagreement you had in the past makes what should be your *best* day feel like the *worst* day. I can't tell you how many birthdays ended with me crying myself to sleep. It almost got to the point where I dreaded any day that put the attention on me. I felt like hiding out on the sidelines was my only option so others wouldn't get jealous of the attention I received.

Doubting your worth or feeling less than. Maybe this is a feeling that your partner is purposefully creating. To recognize this, you must know and feel deep inside that you are not what is being said *about* you or *to* you. You are not those words. Your self-esteem muscle must strengthen during this time to help you to push back on this type of control. As Daddy would often say, "If someone is pointing a finger at you, there are four more pointing back at them." In other words, don't let the words of others hurt you when you know the truth. *You* know *you*.

Feeling guilty about your goals or dreams. Insecurity in a relationship can create fear, and a person who is afraid often lashes out. They can do this with looks, words, and actions. If you have a vision or a dream for something you want to do with your life, there is no reason your partner shouldn't be understanding and supportive of you. Of course, being reasonable, talking it out, and sharing your concerns are all important parts of a loving relationship. The difference in a relationship that loves and supports each other and one that doesn't is like the difference between a homemade cookie and a store-bought one.

Feeling like a puppet being pulled by strings in ways you would never move on your own. Not only are you being pulled by these strings, but any kind gesture that was ever done from what you thought was a place of love is tethered to the act itself, causing guilt. *Aren't you happy with what I have done for you? You should be thankful for everything I have given you.* Exercising our own choices and wishes for what we want in life is one of the greatest parts of being an adult. Too often, we let others make our decisions. We do this for many reasons. Maybe we don't feel strong enough within ourselves, we don't think much of ourselves, or we're afraid to speak up for ourselves. Been there, done that. Believe me, I know it's hard. You're afraid of causing conflict. It's easier to let the other party have their way, but what happens next is what we should fear the most. This looming pressure will eventually build up to a point where it explodes. Watch out! Everything that has a string attached to it will be part of this explosion, and you'll be left picking the shrapnel from your shredded self.

Feeling abandoned during the hardest moments of your life. Often, your loss and your grief become leverage used against you to manipulate you and to fit the other person's selfish narrative. When this would happen to me, I did feel the touch of a hand placed on my back or a hug, but it wasn't from the one I thought would always be there for me. It was from my friends. They were there to help carry some of the weight of my heavy, broken heart. I learned that the one I'd thought had my back the most actually had my back the least.

Early on in my relationships, I didn't pay attention to behaviors that later I would find alarming. Starting out, the red flags were probably a soft pink, so I didn't recognize them, or I wasn't too concerned, thinking a particular word or action was just a one-time thing. As time went on and the relationship grew, the flags became considerably more noticeable, and they began to show up in the brightest reds I'd ever seen. That's why I share this with you, so that you can pay attention to those pale shades of pink before they darken to fire-engine red.

"Your rings are ready to pick up."

"Okay, I'll come by sometime this week," I answered as the word *rings* echoed in my head. The rings had been separated. I was relieved in a way and saddened in another. What once had been put together and beautiful was now going back to the way it had been before, with my mother's ring and mine on their own once again.

I drove to the store, picked up the rings, and put them in my purse. While I was paying at the register, the jeweler came over and hugged me. It was an unexpected but appreciated gesture. Compassion isn't absent from humanity; sometimes, it's just absent from those we choose to put our trust in. Sometimes, those who should be there for us the most are there for us the least. The love that *should* have our back ends up turning its back on us. That's hard to swallow.

When I got into my car, I got the rings out to take a closer look. There they were—my wedding ring and Momma's wedding band. I put my wedding ring back in the bag, but I decided to try Momma's ring on my right hand. It was a wide, gold band with an inscription that read *Joe and Sue 1-10-70*. It fit perfectly.

Not wanting to take any chance on losing it, I took it off and tucked it back in the bag, safe in my purse. I took my wedding ring out and placed it back on my hand one more time. I needed complete closure before putting it away for good. I needed to see it once again on the hand it had called home for the past twelve years. As the tears fell, I knew this ring didn't feel right anymore. It had never felt completely right.

When I started my car, "Wrapped Around Your Finger" by the Police was playing: "Staring at the ring around your finger . . ." I sat there motionless, in shock, speechless, jaw-dropped. The song continued to play: "I know what you're up to just the same . . ." I quickly took the ring off and put it back in the bag. Sitting there in the parking lot, I googled the meaning of the lyrics, and it was exactly what I'd thought. Told from the point of view of an apprentice who finally gets fed up with the way he's been treated by his boss, or leader, the song transitions toward the end, changing from "I'll be wrapped . . ." to "You'll be wrapped . . ." In other words, the "young apprentice" eventually escapes his controlling relationship and frees himself. I will never forget the moment I listened to that song while sitting in the jewelry store parking lot, taking my wedding ring off my finger for the very last time.

Don't settle for a relationship just because it's comfortable or because you're too frightened to try life on your own. The sacrifice will cost you more than you should be willing to pay. Ultimately, the sacrifice is *you*. And you deserve more. You deserve all the happiness and fulfillment you were created to have.

Eventually, the place you find is a place you will never leave. It's a place inside that is you and only you. Once you get there, you will never let it go. It took me a long time, almost fifty years, to find it. The most precious gifts in my life, like my daughter, also came with some of the harshest lessons. The most important thing I can do for her now is to show her what an independent woman—one who is also a child of God—can do with her life to help others. No one can love you like God can. It's impossible. But His love can show you how to love yourself. That's the me I have fallen in love with. That's the me I'm most proud of.

Freewriting Exercise

When I was a high school English teacher, I would start each class with a "freewrite." This was a ten-minute timed writing exercise where my students could get anything they wanted out of their head and onto the page. It was not graded. It was not shared. At the end of the exercise, if a student wanted to share their freewrite, they could, but those who didn't could either keep it or take it to my shredder, which was placed at the front of the classroom.

This was a great way to let my students vent their feelings early in the class, and it can help you mentally free your brain from anything that may be bothering you. Get it out of your head and on the page!

8

Everything on the Buffet

We heal when we have hope.

—Theo Boyd

I LOVE A GOOD BUFFET. I always have. Luby's cafeteria was a favorite place for Daddy, and I find myself combing Texas for a Luby's whenever the opportunity presents itself. Who doesn't love seeing all kinds of delicious foods lined up, waiting for you to choose whatever you want? Daddy never stuck to the preset menu, where you select one entree and two sides. He just started going down the line, filling up his tray until it couldn't hold any more, and then saying, "Well, I guess that's all I'll git."

Hope is kind of like a buffet line. Once you start seeing the divine signs of hope in your life—in both big and small things—you start to see them everywhere. It's like you're my Daddy walking down the buffet line, the signs piling up on one after another, and at the end of the line, you realize you're carrying a tray full of abundance, a large helping of hope.

Some signs have taken years for me to see, while others I saw right away, even immediately after my loss.

After Momma's accident, I worked hard to picture what life would look like moving forward. I tried to make sure Daddy would be okay, worked to get back in the groove at my teaching job, and attempted to piece together a failing marriage. I had my hands full, and it was in those hands that a precious little gift would come visit night after night.

The gift started visiting me very early in my grief. Just a few days before Momma's funeral, I was sitting on the little bench outside my parents' home. It was late in the day, and I was crying. There was so much going on with the funeral preparations and the visitors, and I had just gotten back from the emergency room for my own injury, with several stitches to show for it.

As I sat there drinking a glass of sweet tea someone had dropped off, I felt something on my bare foot. I gasped and jumped, spilling some of the tea from my glass. I looked down, ready to find something horrid and preparing to scream and run back into the house. But what I saw was the most beautiful butterfly I'd ever seen. Mostly black, its wings were outlined in a smoky blue that faded into a lighter shade of blue and softly blended into its black body.

As I stared at this creature, my body began to calm itself. I went from shaking to stillness. I tried to sit there carefully, motionless, watching the butterfly on my foot. She didn't move at all, but I didn't think she would stay very long. I didn't want to scare her away, so I gently reached over to pick up my phone and take a picture. I took one photo, then another, and another. She wasn't going anywhere. Eventually, I became so comfortable with her and she with me that I reached down to touch her. Very softly, I used my index finger to brush against the right side of her scalloped edge. She didn't leave; she wasn't scared. She sat so gently on my foot, like a cat that had found a soft place to rest purring from contentment. I found it so odd that this butterfly had come to sit with me in that moment. She didn't stay long, maybe three or four minutes, but our connection was so strong it felt like forever.

The next day while I was at the funeral home, I was given an envelope filled with some of the programs that would be distributed for Momma's visitation and funeral. Without looking at the contents, I put the envelope in my purse. When I got back to the house where Daddy and others were gathering and visiting, I put the envelope on Daddy's desk so he could look at it later. I didn't want to show him the program with lots of people gathered around, as I knew it would make for another difficult moment, sure to bring him—and all of us—to tears.

As the day wore on, people started to leave, and I decided to take a shower. When I got out of the shower, I heard Daddy crying. "Oh, Sue! You're here. You're here with us."

I called out, "Is everything okay?"

My sister answered, "Yes, Thelizabeth, come see this."

I quickly dried off, threw on my robe, and followed the sound of their voices. "What? What is it?"

Daddy held up the program from the funeral home. He and my sister must have seen the envelope and opened it while I was in the shower. On the front cover, below my mother's picture and birth and death dates, was the image of a beautiful butterfly. She was lighter in color than the one that had visited me, but she had the same shape and the same dark black velvet backdrop.

Looking at me, my sister exclaimed, "That's the same butterfly I saw at the gas station yesterday!"

"What?"

"I saw this butterfly yesterday while I was getting gas, and she was injured and couldn't fly. I picked her up and laid her gently on the curb away from any traffic. I was crying because it was so crazy—I'd never seen a butterfly like this before. I wondered if it was Momma." As my sister explained her encounter, Daddy sat crying, while I stood there in awe with my tear-filled eyes closed, trying to picture it all. We all gathered around Daddy's desk, each feeling our own sentiment in that unforgettable moment.

"I saw that butterfly too," I said softly through my tears.

"WHAT?" Daddy asked.

"I saw this butterfly yesterday evening, while I was sitting outside on your bench. She stayed on my foot for a long time. It was the same butterfly as this one, but just in a blue color. Here, I took a picture."

As we looked at my picture, we smiled, cried, and found comfort through our pain. We were overjoyed that this butterfly had found us. And there she was on the program, too, which none of us had chosen.

"Daddy, Momma is telling us she's okay," I said softly.

"Yes, she is. She sure is. Oh, Sue, my beautiful Sue," Daddy said, as he continued to sort through the emotions that were running high.

From that moment on, we were all a little more aware of our surroundings. I remember my daughter calling me a few weeks later to tell me she was afraid to kill a fly in her kitchen in case it was Nanny. I thought about that for a minute and said, "Reagen, you can kill the fly. Your

Nanny wouldn't dare use a fly to reach out to us after she spent her entire life swatting them away from her homemade pies." We enjoyed a laugh over the phone together, which we hadn't done in a while.

I stayed with Daddy for about six weeks after the accident, and even though our grief was painful and strong, we had glimpses of hope through our shared emotions and anything that reminded us of Momma. I will never forget the precious time we had together, watching *The Winds of War* each night with Robert Mitchum and Ali MacGraw. It was one of his and Momma's favorites, and Daddy couldn't believe I had never seen it. It was a good war drama with a romantic spin, and it was nice to have something to look forward to watching each night. We also pulled out old DVDs of *Family Ties,* the funny '80s television show we had always watched as a family. I will never forget hearing Daddy's laugh over Michael J. Fox's character, Alex P. Keaton, and his love of economics and money. I still watch the show when I want to laugh or when I need to remember Daddy's laugh.

As the weeks passed by, I eventually started leaving Daddy at home alone. He gave me permission to do so, and I knew it was time. My marriage was falling apart, which I think Daddy knew before I did. We both had to find a way to keep going on with our lives. However, moving back home, returning to the classroom, and trying to settle back into the life I'd once had was harder than I realized it would be. Each evening, I would sit on our back porch, looking out at the farm and trying to remember what life had been like before the accident, before the affair, back when I was truly happy. *Will it ever get better? Will I be able to do this?*

As I sat there with my heavy questions, I barely noticed a butterfly flying around my head, but I was too consumed by my thoughts to give it much attention. She began to flutter in front of me, as if saying, *Look at me. I'm here.* Once I gave her my full attention, she landed on my right hand. I raised my hand very slowly to get a better look at her, being careful not to move a muscle. Her wings were painted in the softest shades of brown with varying dots of black. Not as large as the blue butterfly that had paid me a visit in my parents' front yard, this one was small, dainty, fragile. She had a gentleness about her, delicately dancing as she made her way up and down my arm. Her touch was so light and soft, but I could still feel her.

After about five minutes, I took a few photos of her with my cell phone. Just like with the blue butterfly, there was a connection between us. We were both aware of each other's existence. Once she flew away, I thought, *This has never happened to me before.* I knew these close encounters with butterflies were Momma letting me know that everything was going to be okay, and that she was okay.

The next day, I came home after school and went right out to the back porch. It was my favorite time of day, sitting out there, watching Manly sniff around for something to chase in the flower beds, while I rested my body and brain. I hadn't thought any more about the butterfly visit that had happened just the day before—until it happened again. It could have been a different butterfly that looked exactly like the first one, but I like to think it was the same one. She came back into my space, floating in for another visit as if to say, *Hello, I'm here with you always. It will all work out.*

My evenings on the back porch continued through the fall of 2019. Every night for almost three weeks, the butterfly came to sit with me, displaying her beauty. She showed me that life is truly beautiful, and we must enjoy every moment we have together. I thought of nothing else when that butterfly was connecting with me, nothing else but this magical encounter. She reminded me how to be present. She brought a smile to my face each and every time.

In the book *Proof of Heaven,* Dr. Eben Alexander, a neurosurgeon, becomes very ill and dies for a time. On the cover of his book is a little black butterfly with hues of blue, just like the one that first visited me. It caught my eye right away, as I had never seen this color of butterfly before Momma's death. As Dr. Alexander takes us with him on his journey through Heaven, he describes the most fascinating scenes, and I can only imagine the overwhelming beauty:

> *. . . a beautiful girl with high cheekbones and deep blue eyes. . . . We were riding along together on an intricately*

> *patterned surface, alive with indescribable and vivid colors—the wing of a butterfly. In fact, millions of butterflies were all around us—vast fluttering waves of them, dipping down into the greenery and coming back up around us again . . . a river of life and color, moving through the air.*[11]

Since I first read them, these words have never left me. Can you imagine riding on the wing of a butterfly? How magical, mysterious, and completely magnificent! It's like a perfectly planned buffet at a five-star resort, but with thousands of species of butterflies in various shapes and sizes. No matter where you look, they are there for you to enjoy in a kaleidoscope of colors.

I found everything I needed from these little butterfly visits and reminders. They were my reassurance that everything was going to be okay. I didn't need to worry about the small things. I didn't have to decide what part of life I was going to focus on or what I had to do next. I could choose a little of this and a little of that—a helping of hope mixed in with a serving of sorrow. I could have it all, the entire buffet. I could cling to what was clinging to me. God had my attention, and I was mesmerized. He was giving me the answers I needed, in His time.

It's been about a year since my last butterfly visit, but I know it will happen again. The brown butterfly has come to see me twice since Daddy died. The dance was the same, and the connection just as strong. I haven't seen the blue butterfly again, but I know she is there. I know Momma and Daddy were showing me they are okay. They are with each other and will forever be riding on the wings of butterflies.

Think Points

- How do you picture Heaven? What do you see?

- Have you encountered any visits from nature, such as an animal or insect like my butterfly? Describe it here.

Do grief and hope, and all the other feelings in the mix, feel like a buffet to you? How would you describe the buffet of emotions you are experiencing right now?

....

....

....

....

....

....

....

....

....

....

....

9

Well-Done

Hope is always there, waiting for you.
—Theo Boyd

Rib-eye or New York strip?

Our first date had been one to remember. I received a text from Ronnie Joe. Normally, I like my steaks prepared medium, but I smiled as I wrote back.

Rib-eye—over easy 

I was nervous, almost jittery. This would be our first time meeting in person, and I could feel the butterflies. This time they were dancing in my stomach, my mind jumping around thinking of all the *what ifs. What if I'm not ready yet? What if I've misread the signs? What if this is just a waste of time?* My hands were getting clammy, so I took a deep breath and told myself that if it went well, I would have made a friend, and if not, then I could think about trying again later. At the very least, it was a good feeling to be putting on makeup and fixing my hair for a dinner date and not just taking my dog on a walk, as much as I love taking my Manly out.

I texted my friend Carol that I was going to meet the farmer for dinner, and she wrote back right away.

Even if it doesn't work out, it will show you hope.

I hadn't thought of it like that, but she was right. I felt hopeful. For the first time in a long time, I was excited about something.

I took some time picking out what I would wear. Ronnie Joe had asked me out for dinner, but he had made it clear it wasn't a date. Even so, I wanted to look casual and cute but comfortable. I chose capri jeans and a cream-colored ribbed tank top with a light yellowish brown floral blouse with tiny daisies on top. *Not a date,* I told myself, feeling good about my understated choice of clothing that was both pretty and practical.

Ronnie Joe sent me his location, which was about twenty-five minutes away. I put on my favorite songs from the '80s and headed out to enjoy the drive. Little did I know I would enjoy this drive for the next couple of years, and I still do.

When I got close to my location, I pulled over to check my lip gloss and send him a quick text.

3 minutes away!

His reply made me laugh.

I'm hyperventilating. Come to the back door.

I bet you say that to all the girls. 

I was nervous, but I looked good, or at least I thought so. I had sent my fairy blonde-mothers a few quick pics of what I was wearing, asking if it looked okay. They all gave me the thumbs-up and encouraged me to go, get out there, and make a new friend.

When I got to the destination, my location got messed up a little, and I drove right by Ronnie Joe's house. I saw someone outside waving as I passed by. I laughed out loud and quickly put my car in reverse. As I pulled into his driveway, I saw him standing there waiting for me. I grabbed my container of carefully sliced cantaloupe, which I'd taken extra time to cut up perfectly. I figured since he was a farmer, he would appreciate the precision. I threw my purse over my shoulder and walked toward him.

"Hey, how are you?" were his first words to me as I looked into his eyes. "Hey," I said back, and we hugged each other. I'm a hugger anyway, but this hug felt different. It was sweet, soft, yet strong. It was the touch I had missed, a touch from someone other than a girlfriend.

"You smell like home," he said, as his nose brushed slowly by the few pieces of hair that were pulled back by my sunglasses. I didn't know quite what to think of that statement, but I was happy to finally meet him in person, and the feeling I had was new and exciting. In those first few moments, my feelings of anxiety began to fade. I felt like I was back home. It was an emotion that washed over me in an instant. It felt the same as when a wave of grief washed over me, but this time it was a wave of hope.

Ronnie Joe was a sign I didn't know I'd been searching for—a sign that I could hope again. *What are the chances that he and I would meet and be so perfectly matched?* Because of his hearing loss, it's inherent that I face him while speaking, and because of Momma, I naturally did this from the start. It was as if I had known him my entire life. I just had to open up my heart, pieces and all.

Just like grief, hope comes in many forms. Hope can be found in expecting a new baby or grandbaby. Hope can be found in getting a desirable test result from your doctor. Hope can be found in meeting someone who wants to meet you, or in finding a new friend or love. Hope *can* be found.

Hope is always there, waiting for us.

When we're grieving, it can be hard to look into the future and see anything resembling hope. We are *literally* hopeless. Emotions are very specific in grief. Though we might share some common feelings, our reactions to our experience with grief will also be unique. Grief is heavy and fully loaded with the feelings that none of us ever want to feel: pain, anger, fear, and all the other feelings you see in the Venn diagram shown here, and maybe even some I have left out. The hope side, on the other hand, contains the opposite feelings: positivity, peace, happiness, and more. When we are deep in grief, we can completely lose sight of these feelings and even forget they exist.

The good news, though, is that grief and hope can coexist, especially as we heal. You don't have to choose one over the other. In fact, your brain operates more effectively, and you feel better, if you can hold on to hope when faced with adversity and uncertainty. But hope isn't always a given. You have to work at it, understand it, and recognize it for it to take root in your brain.[12]

Yes, hope takes work. In my darkest hours, I had given up on a happy life. I had resolved myself to a life of "just getting by." Grief had already taken so much, and it was taking away everything I had left. But I also needed my grief. It was a way for me to show and feel love for all I had lost. The greater the loss, the greater the grief—and my pain was so immense that I knew there was love overflowing inside me. I didn't want to let go of the pain. I thought I had to hold the pain in my broken heart, or I would be leaving my loved ones behind, forgetting them.

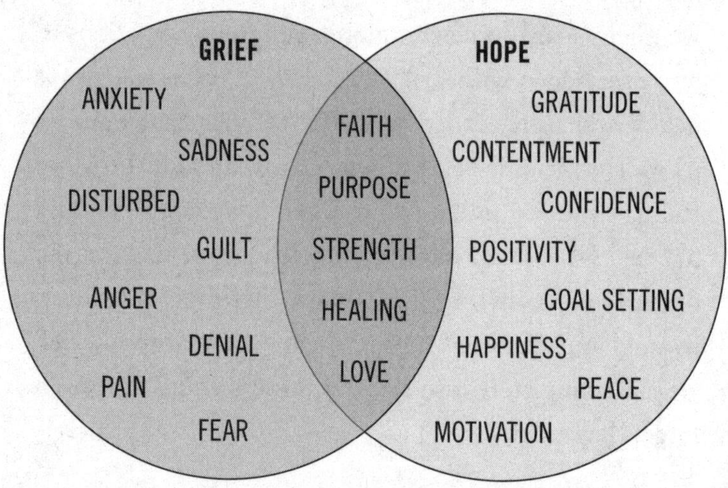

In a sense, I felt that I was betraying them if I *didn't* stay in my sadness. But I came to learn that I could make them proud by finding meaning in my loss, strength in my grief. We can stay *in it* for a time, and that's okay. But as we grow and see the light of hope, we can appreciate the tears that helped water us along the way. And then, it's time to bloom.

I've found that we grow the most in the place where grief and hope intersect, in the *middle* of the diagram. Notice these key words:

Faith
Purpose
Strength
Healing
Love

As we are coming out of painful grief and starting to see the divine signs of hope after loss, these are the words we should focus on. These are the ingredients needed in the recipe of hope. Grief is bitter to taste, but hope is sweet. Hope is pleasing, and it leaves us wanting more.

Once we realize that moving forward isn't leaving those we've lost behind, we can start to experience what God truly wants for us: to love again. To have a well-done kind of life—a juicy steak that has been cooked through but tastes oh-so-good! It took many counseling sessions, talks with friends, and researching on my own to realize that grief isn't a death sentence for those of us who are still living. Grief is a part of us now, but it's evidence of the part that once loved, and more importantly, the part that *can* love again.

I learned about loving again through another sign, one that came in the form of a movie. One of my favorite movies is *Hope Floats*, starring Harry Connick Jr. and Sandra Bullock. I can vividly remember, in January 1999, packing that VHS tape into my hospital bag for the trip I would soon be taking to give birth to my first and only baby, my daughter, Reagen. I thought I could play this movie while I was in labor to distract me from the pain and help with my breathing. Ha! I still laugh about that to this day. I never even got to unpack it from the bag. But even though I didn't get to watch the movie while in labor, I have always kept that VHS tape. I even have the movie saved to my favorites on Amazon, and I watch it quite often.

It wasn't until I started experiencing loss, grief, and eventually hope that I realized how much my life has parallelled this movie. Even crazier, my nephews call me Birdee, a name my sister gave me when we were little. And that's the name of Sandra Bullock's character in the movie—Birdee Calvert.

- ✓ Birdee loses her husband to infidelity.
- ✓ Birdee moves back to her small Texas hometown.
- ✓ Birdee loses her mother suddenly.
- ✓ Birdee watches her father suffer from dementia.
- ✓ Birdee struggles to keep going, get a job, and find her way.
- ✓ Birdee meets a handsome man who accepts her for her and all she's been through.

I *hope* I didn't just spoil this movie for you. You've only had nearly three decades to watch it, so I don't feel too bad. After my losses, one after the other in cataclysmic fashion, my old girlfriends, teacher friends, and of course my fairy blonde-mothers, would come and stay with me. They'd spend a night or two, and each time we'd watch *Hope Floats*. I guess I was wanting to see a similar story to how my life was playing out. Each time we watched, the shock of the parallels would be the same. Except at the time, I hadn't met any *handsome man* yet. I mostly just wanted to see if Birdee survived. And she did. In its own way, the movie helped me realize I could survive too.

In the film, Birdee says, "Beginnings are scary, endings are usually sad, but it's the middle that counts the most. So, when you find yourself at the beginning, just give hope a chance to float up."

She's right. Hope *will* float up. It always does, but you must be there to see it. If you're struggling to see it now, try changing one letter. If you replace the *p* with an *m*, what do you have? *Home*. The *hope* is in the *m-e: me*.

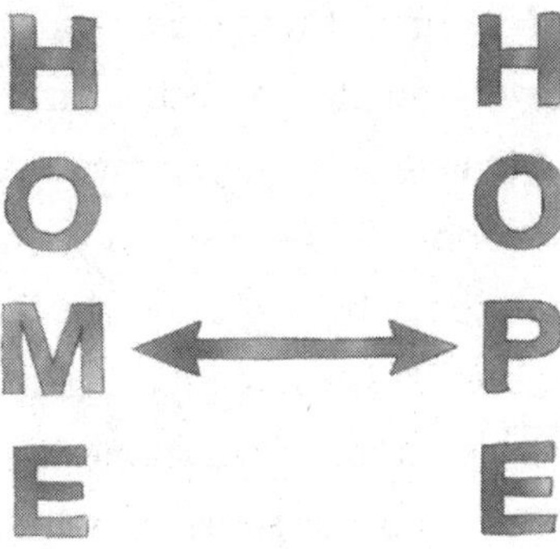

Where do you feel most at home? Is it a place, a person, a feeling you have? Once you can identify what "home" is for you, you will start seeing signs of hope.

I wrote most of my first book at a coffee shop and the library. I was brand-new in my grief, and with the losses coming as fast as the bills arrived in my mailbox, I felt the need to escape my physical home to limit distractions. As time has passed—and with my growing self-awareness through numerous counseling sessions—I began to feel most peaceful and content when I'm home. One thing that I have learned is that home is not just a place, it's also a feeling, a strong one. Home is where I feel most comfortable writing down my intimate thoughts. Sure, I'm still writing some of this book in my favorite coffee shop because I love their specialty coffees, tomato basil soup, and atmosphere, but most of my writing has happened at home, with Manly resting at my feet. Home is a place inside each of us, not just four walls or a building, but a place in our soul that speaks to us, saying we have arrived. It's love. Pure and simple love.

Home is Momma, Daddy, and all the wonderful memories I have growing up on the farm. Home is my grandmother Meme teaching me how to play easy songs on her piano. Home is watching my granddad scoop orange sherbet into my baby blue bowl, all while listening to his laughing box. This was a little box with a switch on its side that was like the sound machines we have now, but when you turned it on there was no white noise or rain sounds—only the hysterical laughter of a man. Granddad would laugh right along with that voice coming from the box, and I loved watching him. Home is all these things and more. But most of all—it's love.

Even now, when I see a redbird and hear its song, I know my loved ones are with me. They are in the smallest of nature's signs. They are in the roadrunner dashing about and in the soft hoot of an owl. These are all gentle reminders that the people who mean the most to me were once here, and their spirits and love remain.

Ronnie Joe and I spent that evening talking, laughing, and eating. He gave me a tour of his home, which had belonged to his grandparents and that he was in the final phase of remodeling. It was a farmhouse that smelled like bread baking in the oven and black-eyed peas on the stove. He grilled rib-eye steaks for us while we sat outside on his patio talking. Neither one of us was looking at the time nor paying attention to anything outside of each other, when I started to smell something and noticed smoke rising behind him.

"Is something burning?" I asked softly, not wanting to impose.

"Oh shit! The steaks!" He jumped up and turned the burners off.

"It's okay. I love my steak well-done."

Well-done. Another perfect way to cook a steak, and a perfect way to describe love after loss. As it turns out, it's even better—a little charred around the edges, but it's warm and tender on the inside. It's been through the fire, and it has survived.

Ronnie Joe hasn't burned any steaks since then, but it sure has been a funny story to share about the night we met. In fact, when I first met Ronnie Joe's son, I told him the story of his dad grilling steaks for me, and he blurted out in shock, "Dad doesn't burn steaks!" I immediately got the biggest smile on my face, feeling so special. He had burned our dinner because I was keeping his attention, and he would rather talk to me than get up to flip those steaks.

He is actually a master in the kitchen, and if I needed any more signs that he was the right guy for me, I could just describe his cooking! Ronnie Joe has a strong Czech heritage, which includes sauerkraut, sausage, and cold beer. Learning the different recipes has been an interesting part of the journey for me. Momma would have loved cooking and baking with him. He has taught me so much about gardening, blanching vegetables, and achieving a farm-to-table meal with a taste that brings me back home, every time.

Daddy would have loved him for his black-eyed peas. Daddy always planted "a little patch" of black-eyed peas that was usually around three acres. When you're carrying a bushel basket in the hot sun with bugs flying around and sweat running down your face, three acres is anything but "a little patch." But homegrown black-eyed peas versus store-bought canned ones is as big of a contrast as a hundred-degree day is to a twenty-degree day. They taste real, fresh, and just damn good.

The first time Ronnie Joe cooked black-eyed peas for one of our meals, I took a bite and started crying. They were happy tears, as this was a taste of something I never thought I'd enjoy again. I could see Daddy and Momma sitting there with me, enjoying the peas they had planted, picked, and shelled together. They tasted like home.

Think Points

Do you ever feel homesick? How do you overcome this feeling?

Is there a food that brings back a wonderful memory for you? What is it, and what does it remind you of?

10

Made to Order

Open my eyes that I may see
glimpses of truth thou hast for me.
Place in my hands the wonderful key
that shall unclasp and set me free.[13]
—Clara H. Scott

I SAW NANNY."

"What?" my sister asked.

"I saw Nanny with a baby," her four-year-old son, Henry, repeated in his soft, sweet voice.

It was about two months after Momma's death when my sister had called me rather urgently. She explained that Henry had been playing in his room before walking out to tell her that he'd seen our mom, his Nanny, with a baby.

When Momma died on July 29, 2019, she died on the same day as a baby boy from the community named Finn. They were together at the same funeral home. Momma wasn't alone in death. She had this baby, and he had her. So when I heard that Henry had seen his Nanny with a baby, it made complete sense to me. My heart simultaneously felt full and broken, remembering that she wasn't here with me but knowing she wasn't alone. I felt the fullness of the blessing to have had this woman as my mother, and I was happy that she was comforting this baby, but I also felt the brokenness of realizing I would never again feel her physical touch on this earth. The arms that would wrap around me whenever I needed them were now wrapped around this baby.

It's so important for us to understand that although our loved ones may have left us here on earth, they still show up in the signs if we're open to seeing them. This sign from my nephew gave me a peaceful feeling, knowing Momma's energy and spirit were still surrounding us.

I've reached out to Finn's mom, Taylor, since I released *My Grief Is Not Like Yours,* and we have shared an ineffable number of tears and a mutual love that *my* Momma and *her* baby had each other. They were together at the funeral home during the days and nights until they were both peacefully laid to rest on August 3, 2019, with their services following each other. I will never forget seeing Momma with this baby next to her in the newspaper, their obituaries side by side, just like their bodies were on their last few days and nights on earth. That image is one that will last forever for me, so sweet yet also so painful—bittersweet. I'm thankful to be able to see the beauty in this—the proof that God is good and that "all things work together for good" (Romans 8:28 KJV). In the darkest of days, God brought His light in by giving Momma a baby to hold and giving Finn the comfort of being held.

One afternoon, while I was searching through different grief books online, I stumbled upon a children's book written by an author who had the same name as Finn's mother. *Could this be her? She never mentioned this before. Did Taylor write a grief book for children?* I immediately ordered the book—*My Loved One Is in Heaven*—and sent Taylor a text.

It turns out she had written it! While I wrote a grief book for adults when I lost my mother, she wrote a grief book for children when she lost her baby boy. There are no coincidences here. I'm so grateful to Mr. Fine—the best funeral director on the planet—for bringing us together, and most of all for placing the baby next to Momma each night. God was at work, placing us all exactly where He wanted us to be.

A few days later, the book arrived. I couldn't wait to read it. The illustrations were so peaceful and purposeful. As I turned the pages, I saw something that made my heart skip a beat. It was another one of those moments where you remember exactly where you were when it happened, a flashbulb moment. My jaw dropped open; my eyes stared at the page without blinking.

In the picture, the illustrator had drawn a child's bedroom. Hanging on the wall, there it was: "We know that all things work together for good to those who love God. Romans 8:28." The verse! Daddy's verse. There are 31,102 verses in the Bible, and here was the same one that had become the theme for my life, the verse I used in my grief book, the verse that kept appearing since Daddy's death on June 19, 2022.

There are several places I would see it that made sense—a church bulletin, a sympathy card from someone who attended the service—but to see it here was a sign from Heaven. My arms were completely covered with tiny goosebumps. I felt a tingle in my spine, and my breathing had become shallow. *Does Taylor also understand the importance of this verse after her loss?* As a mother who had lost her precious baby boy, she was grieving but still believed God worked all things for good.

I immediately took a picture of the illustration and sent it to my closest friends. *Can you believe this?* I asked.

I reached out to Taylor after reading her book and explained the amazement I'd felt when I saw the illustration. I told her that this verse had proven true throughout my grief journey, and she said it had resonated with her as well.

One more little sign that spoke to both of us was my dad's name, Joe Bob. She told me this name had really stood out to her when she read my book because Finn's favorite uncle shared the same name—Joe Bob. It's a rather unique name, believe it or not. There are many two-name combinations in the South, but seeing these particular two together was unusual.

In my lifetime, I have probably read through the Bible *at least* twenty times. Growing up in the church, with Daddy leading Bible studies and services, we would study one chapter at a time until we reached the end of the Bible, and then we'd start over again. Unfortunately, back then I didn't pay attention like I should have. So, having been pushed down into the dirt after my tragic losses, I started to dig a little, hoping to find a way up and out. I have all of Daddy's study books, Bible commentaries, and his personal Bible that has more handwritten notes in the margins than a recipe that's been handed down for generations. Daddy's handwriting was uniquely terrible, so deciphering his words is a challenge. But if anyone can do it, I can.

"And we know that all things work together for good to them that love God, to them who are the called according to his purpose" (Romans 8:28 KJV). Notice the words *all things* in this verse. Did you know those two words appear eighteen times in the Bible? *What is God's purpose in these words? Why is He grouping "all things" together? Does it cover everything, like a blanket statement?* These were all questions I asked myself for many weeks after Daddy's death. But when God says "all things," He means *all things.* It has taken me some time to fully grasp this, but with prayer for understanding and by seeing first-hand the people who have been moved by the words I wrote in *My Grief Is Not Like Yours,* I know exactly what God means by "all things."

The way Momma died and the way that everything has happened in my life, I find myself often in disbelief. *How could God have made all this good? How could Daddy, who served God his entire life with every fiber of his being, have been the cause of this horrible accident? Why did my counselor die when I needed her the most? How could my husband leave me in my darkest hour?* I questioned God. I was angry. I almost lost my faith, but God never lost me. He held me and picked me up, wiped my tears away, and showed me the way forward. My passion, the meaning in my life, is more rewarding than anything I have ever done. Sure, I've loved the jobs I've had in the past, but the job God has set before me now is one that comes from complete desperation, isolation, and devastation. Life-changing events have shaped me, and I am stronger now to go out and help those who, like me, are suffering in their sadness. I am here to share my story and the pieces of my broken heart, which God has filled with hope.

Along with an asterisk to mark the verse, Daddy had drawn a line under the words *called* and *purpose*. In *The Bible Knowledge Commentary* by John F. Walvoord and Roy B. Zuck, we learn that the Holy Spirit lives inside each believer.[14] With the Holy Spirit living inside us, God summons the "called" to the work of bringing us together for the ultimate good and solidifying our love of Him and His love for us.

When I was planning Daddy's funeral, I instructed my cousin David, the minister guiding the service, to use Romans 8:28. It had come to me like a bolt of lightning. I blurted out to David, "Romans 8:28, Romans 8:28, Romans 8:28," and insisted he use that verse in the service. After the funeral, he told me, "It was difficult to write the sermon for Joe Bob's service with that verse, but after I did, I had so many people tell me they would never think of that verse the same way."

Christians are significantly more likely than non-Christians to see the value in having a purpose for their lives.

After seeing the verse appear numerous times over the past six years, I no longer believe it's simply the Baader-Meinhof phenomenon (a cognitive bias that causes people to notice something more after learning about it). It's God. It's His hand in my life. It's His Divine Plan for me, Thelizabeth Boyd. From the moment I was created, God has had a plan for my life, and now I feel like I can see it. I can understand it. The best part is that He is using me, and my life, to help others. I'm so blessed and honored to have been *called* to carry out His purpose through the story of Joe Bob and Sue. He has a purpose for your life too. Don't ever doubt that. You are here for a reason. His perfect plan is made to order, just for you.

And hope maketh not ashamed;
because the love of God is shed abroad in our hearts
by the Holy Ghost which is given unto us.
—Romans 5:5 (KJV)

In all the work I've done with *My Grief Is Not Like Yours*, sharing my story and giving some form of guidance to broken hearts, I never thought too much about what was happening all around me—well, until the signs started to float in. Since my grief began, I've experienced a heightened awareness of death and what it means for those of us still here, alive on earth. Losing someone we love is one of the hardest things we as humans will ever experience, if not *the* hardest. I mean, I *did* write a grief book, so yes, I think a lot about life, death, and what happens next.

When the signs started coming, one after another, I couldn't discount them. *Is it Momma? Is it Daddy? Is it God?* After hearing that my nephew "saw Nanny," I thought she must have been an angel coming to visit him. After a little self-reflection, I realized I had been concerned about how to help others by sharing my story and these signs, but I'd never stopped to educate myself on one very important possibility, a question I should have been asking myself all along: *Is it an angel?*

After Momma died, and again after Daddy died, I thought of them both as angels. I often told friends and family that I just knew Momma had become head of the angel choir now that her hearing had been completely restored in Heaven. She could now hear music, and I was certain that her new voice was pure and angelic.

Memories of music with Momma are few.

"Momma, why aren't you singing?"

"I don't sing good. I can't hear the music," she would reply with a look of shame.

I remember her trying to sing to satisfy my childlike curiosity, but it wasn't like any singing I had ever heard before. It was her familiar voice, but she couldn't hear melody or pitch, so it was like she was speaking it out. I later felt bad about pushing her to sing in church, but I was so young. I didn't fully understand her deafness until years later.

Music has always played a major role in my life. I took piano lessons most of my childhood, and I played for church and often played when Daddy just had a request to hear music around the house. From junior high band to high school drill team, music has always been a part of me, forever enriching my life. I don't think there is one song from the '80s that I don't love. This era shaped me, and I continue to pay for SiriusXM just to hear their *80s on 8*.

I have thought many times about what it's like now for Momma. *What sounds is she hearing for the first time? What is the music like in Heaven?* I love to picture it, or at least what I think it's like.

The Venue

My young nephew recently asked, "What's the language in Heaven?" This question didn't surprise any of us, as Henry is quite curious when it comes to spirituality. As with most thought-provoking questions, my mind digs deeper until I eventually grab a pen and paper.

With both my parents having left this earth, I often wonder what it's like for them now. More specifically, what does Heaven sound like?

My mother was deaf. When she was only eighteen months old, she became sick with a very high fever that lasted several days, and as a result, she lost her hearing. Later in life, she wore a hearing aid, but even that would only allow her 5 percent of the sounds around her.

Momma never heard the melody of music, the harmony of voices singing, or the wind whistling through a window gap on a cold winter day. She said any tone or pitch of music sounded like a loud, rumbling noise. When sitting in church on Sunday mornings singing hymns, she would use her index finger to follow along in the songbook, reading Daddy's lips to figure out where we were in the verse or chorus.

Despite Momma's deafness, my parents were dedicated to making music a meaningful part of my life. I was enrolled in piano lessons at the age of four. Momma drove me to lessons twice a week for thirteen years, yet she never heard a note. Daddy would take me with him each year when the Fort Worth Symphony Orchestra came to a nearby town. We would sit and enjoy the different sounds of the instruments as they performed the most difficult pieces effortlessly. On our drive home, we would discuss the songs we loved the most and why.

I have often pictured Heaven as an endless music fest, with a different band and singer on every corner. All the greats are there, and the venue keeps adding more to the lineup. Any time I hear that a well-known singer has died, I picture them getting set to debut their music on a new stage in Heaven.

Through the years, we have lost many great musicians, vocalists, singers, and songwriters. I'm sure Heaven is filled with the sound of music from all genres. Some of the latest to be showcased are Jimmy Buffett, with his tropical island sounds, and Charlie Robison, the country singer/songwriter from Texas. I can picture the crowds going wild with the announcement of each new act, and every ticket holder has a VIP seat.

In the sweet by and by, you hear it all, playing on a perfection loop. "When Doves Cry," and you "Hear That Lonesome Whippoorwill," "That'll Be the Day" "I Will Always Love You." The "Trip Around the Sun" has "We've Only Just Begun" while you go "Walkin' After Midnight" down "Sunset Boulevard." "Are You Lonesome Tonight?" plays softly "From a Distance" and on "Silver Wings" you find there "Ain't No Mountain High Enough," so you "Let It Be." Opening acts of choirs filled with angels singing "Amazing Grace" and "When We All Get to Heaven" fly above the crowds to announce each performance. "I Can Only Imagine"!

My mother now has a front-row seat to all the music she missed while trapped in silence here on earth. With Daddy by her side, they are both in a place where they will never grow old, and all the troubles of the world are forgotten. They are in everlasting love, surrounded by melodious music, and you can't beat the venue!

After my parents died, I was quick to label them both as angels in Heaven. The truth is, while they are in Heaven, they are only *in* the presence of God's angels; they are *not* angels themselves. I share this with you because it's very important to understand that angels have a specific duty and responsibility to God. They are there to assist Him. *We* are not angels. In fact, the more I read about angels, the more I realize that becoming an angel would actually *not* happen because angels and Christians have different purposes for God. This is your mini sermon from a preacher's daughter:

When you are a Christian, this means that you have accepted Christ into your heart, understanding that it is only through Jesus that we can have access to God. What I mean by *access* is having a relationship with Him through prayer and the Holy Spirit. Christians believe that God sent His son, Jesus, to earth. Jesus was crucified on a cross as a sacrifice for our sins, and after three days, He rose again, and later ascended to Heaven, leaving us with the Holy Spirit. He promises to come again to bring all believers to be with Him in Heaven forever. This is what is called the *blessed hope*. Hallelujah!

God made him who had no sin to be sin for us,
so that in him we might become
the righteousness of God.
—2 Corinthians 5:21

In the book *Angels, Satan, and Demons,* Dr. Robert Lightner uses specific Scripture to explain the angel world. I don't know what compelled me, but I was on Amazon one evening perusing different things, and I just typed in "books by Dr. Robert Lightner." One title really stood out to me, so I ordered it.

Dr. Lightner was a great friend of our family. He and Daddy met when I was about three years old, and he visited our little church as a guest pastor numerous times throughout the years. He, his wife, Pearl, and their three daughters would come down for a Sunday sermon, lunch, and a long afternoon visit. Momma went all out for lunch when the Lightners came over, and I remember Daddy being thankful he had a Sunday off, which was always much needed.

Daddy and Dr. Lightner would sit for hours discussing the Bible and different Scriptures and telling funny stories, while finishing off some of Momma's banana pudding, which was Dr. Lightner's favorite dessert. They both had a strong sense of humor and an even stronger love of God's Word.

One time, Daddy mentioned needing some help on the farm if Dr. Lightner had any time off. Well, he came down on a weekday, wearing farmwork clothes. We had never seen Dr. Lightner in anything except a nicely tailored suit, so seeing him in boots and jeans was almost comical, but he looked like a man ready to do a hard day's work. "That was one of the best days I ever had," I heard Daddy recall many times over the years.

What the preacher and the farmer discussed, while out in the field and around the kitchen table, which was covered with Momma's home cooking, would probably baffle most. I remember overhearing their conversations in the living room, and they were deep. I bet their talk out in the dirt, in God's creation, must have been authentically pure and purposeful. They had such a great time working together, and now I wish I could have been out there with them. But at the time, I was a teenager, and the last place I wanted to be was working out in the field when

I didn't have to. I wish I were there right now because I have so many questions for both of them.

It seemed that just when I needed answers to something, the person I wanted to ask was taken from me, gone forever. This showed me that I needed to look for the answers myself and rely on the written word of those who had gone before me and were authorities on the Scriptures. Most of all, it shows me that I need to pray that God reveals the answers to me, and that I am open to receiving them.

I believe that finding Dr. Lightner's book was one of the many ways God has guided me to discover more answers. In *Angels, Satan, and Demons,* Dr. Lightner clearly lays out the facts about angels, explaining what we often confuse or misinterpret about them.

The English word *angel* comes from the Hebrew word *mal ak* and the Greek word *angelos.* Both of these words mean "messenger." Angels are God's messengers, God's ministering spirits. They were created by God. Often, they will take on the form of a human body. When I read this, I felt so comforted and validated. I also immediately thought of the song "Angels Among Us" recorded by the band Alabama. Angels took on human form all throughout the Bible, so why would we think they stopped doing this? They were created to fulfill God's purposes, and they often descended to earth in physical form to help with human challenges.

> Angels can never experience salvation by God's grace. In heaven, Christians will have glorified bodies. But

> holy angels have never been glorified because they have never sinned. In the resurrection believers will become *like* angels to some degree (Matthew 22:30), but they will never actually *become* angels.[15]

Angels are among us, protecting us and guiding us. God has created them for this very purpose. I believe it. I feel it. I know it. He always knows what we need. His angels are *made to order,* just for us. I will continue to keep my eyes open so that I can see what *God* has for me. Too often, there is a great concentration or thought given to angels. Don't let the *angels* in your life replace God. He is the one we should be praying to and loving, and *He* is the one who has saved us from this sinful world.

In our commitment to healing, we must be open to the signs around us. This means there may be someone who has just come into your life, someone *God* has placed there, and you consider that person an angel on earth, helping you through a difficult time. Just know that *He* knows who, when, and where to place the pieces in the exact right place for you, and *He* may use angels to help.

Think Points

Do you have a favorite verse from the Bible? Write it down here.

....

....

....

....

....

....

....

....

....

....

Do you have a special *flashbulb* memory, where you remember exactly where you were, how it looked, and how it felt? Describe your memory here.

....

....

....

....

....

....

....

....

....

....

Have you ever experienced an "angel moment"? Describe it here.

....

....

....

....

....

....

....

....

....

....

11

To Go, Please

From the moment you left, I have longed for home.

—Theo Boyd

I'm going to be on a tractor all day.
If you want to ride . . . ?

It didn't take long to reply to Ronnie Joe's text with an enthusiastic:

Yes!!!

My fingers typed out what my heart wanted before my brain reminded me what I was doing. *Can I really do this?*

On the day of Momma's accident, I decided right then and there—I would never drive, ride on, or even be near a tractor again.

And then that resolution was quickly forgotten in one simple text exchange with this farmer I now found myself falling for.

I called one of my fairy blonde-mothers knowing she would completely understand what I was facing.

"What in the world have I just done?" I exclaimed. "I just told Ronnie Joe that I would come ride the tractor with him this afternoon. AAAHHHH!"

"Well, it'll be okay. If you get there and you decide you can't do it, he'll understand." In true fairy blonde-mother fashion, she eased my concerns.

As I drove to the location he'd sent me, I took slow, deep breaths—in through the nose, out through the mouth. I repeated this on the drive as I listened to some calming '80s music.

I can do this. I can. After all, he knows what I've been through, and he wouldn't ask me if he wasn't certain this was safe.

Many times in grief, we just want to eat and run. "*Can I get it to go, please?*" That seems to suit us best. It's hard to face people at times, and it's also hard for people to be there for us when they're uncomfortable around our grief. So it can be much easier to just get it to go. We want to avoid having uncomfortable interactions, talking about feelings, doing anything we don't want to do.

But to find your way to hope and for hope to find you, you must stay. Stay a while. Don't rush. Just go with the flow. If you get the chance to meet someone, or if you have an opportunity that presents itself, don't just push the menu away. You can stay, see if there is something new that you may want to try. *Stay. Pray. Play.*

When I approached Ronnie Joe's field that day, my mind continued to repeat these affirmations. Sure enough, there was the tractor, and it was huge. Daddy's farm equipment consisted of Case IH and International Harvester brands, but what I saw coming toward me was green—John Deere green. I watched as Ronnie Joe made his way through the soil, disturbing it and sending up a cloud of dust, helping to show his position in the field. I reached in my back pocket for my cell phone and started filming. Momma always recorded Daddy in the field with a big camcorder, and I can't imagine what she could have done with the technology we have now. I thought it would be nice to have a recording of my first tractor ride with Ronnie Joe. Even better, he told me later that he didn't have any video that he knew of showing him at work in the field.

I just love pictures and videos of life on the farm. Capturing these moments has become one of my favorite hobbies. I now have hours of video of this farmer and his work. I always tell him it's important so that one day his children and grandchildren will be able to see what he did. And when you set a video to music, it can be so emotional, and sometimes even funny. I've used songs such as "Corn" by Blake Shelton, "American Farmer" by Alabama, and "Take This Job and Shove It" by Johnny Paycheck.

I have another video I made of our first year together. Just as most people in love have "their song," we do too. Ours is "Feels Like Home" by Randy Newman. We love the version sung by Chantal Kreviazuk the best. Ronnie Joe had mentioned it when we first met, but I had never heard it. When he played it for me, we looked at each other in silence. As the song played, he took my hand and led me to the dance floor of his kitchen. We both felt so comfortable with each other. Home was the feeling that each of us had when we were together. For me, this song completes my circle.

As I continued to hold my phone up to capture some of the plowing that day, the tractor came closer, and the line of dust grew. I watched as he slowed to a stop, then tucked my phone into the back pocket of my jeans. I began trudging through the dirt in my tennis shoes. I'd thrown on my older pair, so I didn't care if they got messed up. Trying to walk as gracefully as possible, I waved, wondering exactly how I was going to get up to where he was. About that time, I could see the door of the cab open, and Ronnie Joe began climbing down the steps. With ease, he walked straight toward me.

Handsome and strong, he was easy on the eyes. His five-foot, eleven-inch frame slowly came into focus with each movement through the haze in the air. In his Red Wing boots, he stepped with a purposeful stride, his Wrangler jeans dusting the earth. His skin was sunkissed, soil powdering his chest and arms. He was wearing Oakley sunglasses, and as he got closer, he lifted his cap to run his fingers through his thick hair, which was shaded as richly as clay topsoil. It was like watching the share of a plow cutting through the earth, slowly making straight, deep rows.

"Hey there, how are you?" he said as he hugged me with one arm.

"I'm okay," I replied, relief in my voice. "I didn't know if I could do this."

"Oh, this? You don't need to worry about this thing. You see, it's not a tractor, it's a spaceship," he assured me. We both laughed.

"I'll go first. You just come up behind me," he instructed.

"Okay, got it."

So I did it. I grabbed the railing along the steps, and as I got to the door, he said, "See, you have your own seat. It's called a buddy seat."

As I held back the tears that day, I couldn't decide if they were tears of sadness or a sweet satisfaction my soul had been longing for.

"How are you doing?" he asked, seeming concerned and like he didn't want to add any stress.

I smiled and told him, "I'm doing great, really. I'm happy."

As we traveled back and forth through the field, he explained the technicalities of the machine. I'm sure Daddy wished I would have listened more to him when he talked about farm things, but I think it's normal for children to tune their parents out. Plus, I was a lot younger then. I had Bon Jovi, banana clips, and Jordache jeans on my mind.

The day was coming to an end, the sun being pulled down from the other side, and it was beautiful. As the sky began to turn a soft shade of orange, I knew it was probably time for me to start heading home. I will never forget how the sun looked and how the smell of the air made me feel. I was getting a deep sensation of belonging, like the earth was calling out to me.

It's been over two years now, and riding in the buddy seat is one of my favorite things. I love the look of the land as the tractor plows through it, pushing it, preparing it. The smells are familiar and filled with meaningful memories.

"Thank you for this," I said softly.

"Thank you for saying yes. I didn't think you would come, so when you texted back 'yes' I was thrilled. It was nice to have a buddy today," he said.

As he opened the door, I quickly told him goodbye, but then I noticed he was coming down the steps right behind me.

As my feet reached the bottom and sunk into the soil, I turned to him. "Save my seat for next time?"

"You bet," he replied, his hand slowly tracing up my arm.

He reached out and wrapped both of his arms around my waist. As a burst of wind carried the smell of the season swiftly by, he pulled me in tight. His hands came around to gently cradle my face. Wiping away a small speck of dirt from my cheek, he pulled a few strands of windblown hair away from my eyes. I felt protected in his embrace. With a passion that I had been missing for what felt like years, maybe a lifetime, his lips touched mine. It was soft, sweet, sure, and it was ours. In that moment, I felt that my entire life made sense. I had come full circle, so they say. This farm girl was back where she belonged.

Hope had brought me home.

In thinking about *home* and what that word means to me, I am reminded of a story Daddy would often tell in the pulpit at the closing of a sermon:

> *An old, married missionary couple was flying back home after a long time away ministering to a village in another country. Their son was meeting them at the airport, and about the same time their plane landed, a famous rock star's plane arrived. The airport was filled with reporters, photographers, and hundreds of fans. The son stood alone, waiting for his parents, and when they were reunited, the father said, "What's wrong, son? Why do you look so sad?"*
>
> *He replied, "Dad, Mom, those people should be here, cheering for you and all the work you've done to bring the Word of God to others. All that fanfare and celebration should have been yours today as you arrived home."*
>
> *The dad looked into his son's eyes and with a smile on his face he answered, "But son, I'm not home yet."*

Isn't that beautiful? The next time you feel unnoticed or unappreciated for work you are doing—work that you know is making a difference in the lives of others—remember this story. It always gives me that little dash of hope I need.

For I reckon that the sufferings of this present time are not worthy to be compared with the glory which shall be revealed in us.
—Romans 8:18 (KJV)

My Two Homes

Just another house that's weathered and worn?
Yes it is, but it's also where I was born.

On a cold December's day, back in 1943,
There was old Dr. Treat, some neighbor ladies, and
Of course, my mother and me.

I grew up in this house.
It's where I came to be a man,
With what my daddy taught me and
By my mother's loving, guiding hand.

This house sits idle now and
Probably won't be lived in anymore,
But oh, the memories I have of going
In and out its doors.

Sometimes now, as I look back across the way,
I can remember what did happen
On many a particular day.

These recollections can certainly make me sad,
But because of all my blessings,
They mostly make me glad.

Yes, this old house I'll always love.
It was here that I came to know of
My other home above.

In a rocking chair on my mother's knees,
She told me of God's love and
How Jesus died for me.

Through His redemptive work and resurrection,
There is HOPE for one and all.
We look forward to His soon return when
We will hear that Heavenly call.

I'm certainly not a poet, as I know you'll all agree,
But I wanted you to know
I'm thankful for my home down here and
Especially for the one God has prepared for me.

Written by Joe Bob Boyd
1998

When I was spending a lot of time writing, I would leave my house early in the morning, load Manly up in the car, and then head over to the farm to check on things. It was also a good way to get some exercise in for Manly early in the day so he would allow me the time I needed later to work on writing.

On this particular day, it was a bright blue sky, sun-in-your-face kind of morning when we headed to the farm. I was toying around with the idea of selling my home and getting something smaller, but it hadn't even crossed my mind to move back to the farm.

In fact, I was looking at some other homes in the area where I currently lived but hadn't made any decisions yet. I just didn't know what to do, but I did realize that my life was pretty complicated, and I wanted nothing more than to simplify it. Life was always simple when I went home.

I always knew where the road home would lead me—to warm hugs, warm food, and the warmth of the love that lived there.

As I drove down the road that led to the farm, I turned on the radio to find something energizing that might have the same effect as coffee, since I'd forgotten to bring any with me.

"You get your hands in it, plant your roots in it. . ." the song on the radio began to play. I immediately increased the volume, listening intently to each word as my eyes looked out at the very land that this song was talking about. *"This elm shade, red rust clay you grew up on . . ."*[16]

My eyes flooded with tears, which began to fall faster than I could wipe away. I had my answer. I called Ronnie Joe. "I'm building a house on the farm. I'm going home," I blurted out, sobbing. Hearing the words of this song, I felt like Daddy was right there with me, telling me where I should be. The farm is where I belong. I just needed a little direction, a little push.

68% of grieving Americans believe that moving toward the meaning and purpose in their life has helped them live more of the life they want.

I had plenty of land to build on, but this plan had never even entered my mind until I heard the song's words on this bright morning. I had the original deed to my family's farmland; I just hadn't considered building there. The deed was signed with a quill pen by my great-grandfather,

H. C. (Hugh Caswell) Boyd, on June 20, 1892. I treasure this document and plan to display it in my new home. Yes, I'm building a new home on my family land, on the old Boyd place. I'm moving forward and bringing my memories with me as I continue to work on integrating my grief. It's a beautiful thing when you get back to the place your heart has always been.

I'm going home.

You know you came from it,
And some day you'll return to it.
—"Dirt," Florida Georgia Line[17]

Think Points

Have you allowed yourself to feel hope and love again?

Is there something you have been frightened of since your loss?

Where was your childhood home? Have you been back there recently?

....

....

....

....

....

....

....

....

....

....

....

What does *home* mean to you?

....

....

....

....

....

....

....

....

....

....

....

SPECIAL EXTRAS

FARM-TO-MEMORIES

I COME FROM A RURAL area of Texas. My background noise was not the hustle and bustle of a city, but rather the hum of working tractors and the bold bellows of cattle grazing outside my bedroom window. It's a peaceful place with humble hopes and raw realizations, holding hints of how harsh life can be.

Being blessed to grow up on a farm, I learned how to navigate through life—one road at a time, one memory at a time. Unbeknownst to me, a true constant lying north to south was a skinny stretch of concrete called FM3050. This farmer's passage, running approximately three miles long, wasn't paved until the late 1960s. Before that, it was just dirt, covering all who took its path with red clay and sandy loam soil that comprise this small section of earth.

Named appropriately, these roads allow farmers to go from farm to market, taking goods and produce to peddle in surrounding towns. The bold, white letters, lying across a square, black sign with the shape of Texas nestled in the center, are more than a directional instruction to me. They represent my life held in one space and too often—where the rubber met the road.

We all travel to different places, from childhood to adulthood, standing on the foundation we were given to ground us. In my own life, these little bumps in the road, whether I was speeding over them or dodging around them, have been painful parts of a journey that has strengthened me. Where potholes became craters and ditches became valleys, I learned how to navigate the tough terrain of each road I traveled. Holding the history of the directions my life has taken and mapping out the future with signs of hope, I can appreciate what this road has given me.

It is . . .
the road my great-grandparents settled on in 1890 and would call home.
the road that leads to our family farm and ranch.
the road that brought me home from the hospital.
the road that took me to school.
the road where I had my first kiss.
the road that took me to piano lessons.
the road I crossed to go to church.
the road that held my hopes and dreams.
the road that was my parents' last ride away.
the road my family traveled for over one hundred years,
and the road that brought me home again.

The road of life is anything but straight. We follow it, crooked and curved, the best we can, keeping our eyes set on the path ahead. With age comes wisdom, and we learn that obstructions and detours are painful, purposeful, but possible to maneuver. Holding hope in our hearts, we can see the road ahead more clearly, trusting that our destination will soon be reached. After many years away, I am now going home—taking in every moment, knowing I'm just along for the ride on this farm-to-memories road.

Theo Boyd
Fall 2024

"Where I'm From" Writing Exercise

This is an exercise I always did with my high school students at the beginning of each year. It's a fill-in-the-blank assignment, and it's a rich and unique way to put your memories on the page. I remember reading mine before Thanksgiving lunch in 2017. As someone who was famous for always having a poem, Bible verse, or something I felt was meaningful to read, I would always jump right in after Daddy's prayer with "I have something to read!" For those in the room with hungry stomachs, distracted by the aromas of Momma's delicious food waiting for us, I did my best to be a speedy reader. On this particular occasion, I remember seeing a few tears streaming down Daddy's face, while Momma stood beside me looking at the words as I read them. Here's what I wrote:

Where I'm From

I am from the big and little sissies, and the yellow refrigerator, from Dawn and Campho Phenique.

I am from the white house on the hill and all the farm equipment scattered in the purple and yellow iris flowers and the big cactus in the front yard.

I am from presents on Christmas Eve and naturally curly hair, from Thelma and Elizabeth to make *Thelizabeth* and the Boyds.

From always be a Christian and do things for others. I am from born-again believers, from a daddy in the pulpit singing and me at the piano playing and a mom who could only see it.

I'm from Whitney, from Texas and Great Britain some too, from the best chocolate pies ever made and peanut brittle fresh from the kitchen.

From a daddy in the sandy soil all day and the smell of peanuts in the air, sitting in the truck waiting on a full trailer, and a dog named Trisha always by my side.

I am from the white photo album with small pictures and old, sticky pages. I am from the momma who couldn't hear and piano lessons from Mrs. Bessire.

I am from the old cedar chest and wearing Momma's wedding dress.

To all these I am from—the priceless memories, and they are the many things I am thankful for.

Here's a template for you to try. Be creative! Maybe you can read this to your family one day.

Where I'm From

By: ______________________________

1. I am from _______________ and _______________.
   [specific, ordinary item product or brand name]

2. I am from ________________________________.
   [description of your home]

3. I am from the ______________________________.
   [something you do with your family]

4. I am from ______________ and ______________.
   [family tradition]

5. I am from the ____________ and ______________.
   [family trait]

6. From ________________ and ________________.
   [family last names]

7. I am from ______________ and ______________.
   [something you're told frequently]

8. I am from ______________ and ______________.
   [something that represents your family's beliefs]

9. From ________________ and ________________.
   [where you or your ancestors were born]

10. I am from __________________________________.
   [story about a specific family member]

(Created by George Ella Lyon)[18]

BUSHEL BASKET

I WAS WALKING AT THE farm today, and something caught my eye. I glanced a little closer and saw it.

There, under a tree, all by itself, was a bushel basket. Just beyond the barbed wire, sitting on top of a thin scattering of autumn leaves with the morning sun drying the dew, the basket sat empty and alone.

I thought about how many times I'd heard Daddy say, "Get a bushel basket."

This bushel basket was needed daily around the farm. When I remember my childhood, bushel baskets were always part of the scene.

Sitting. Waiting. Empty. Filled. Constant.

We would fill the baskets with cantaloupe, peas, or pears. Sometimes, Momma would use them as part of her fall decorations.

When Daddy died, I went on a hunt for bushel baskets. I found two, and we filled them with cantaloupe from the grocery store. They created a beautiful scene as we placed them around the base of Daddy's casket.

"Get a bushel basket." Daddy's voice echoed in my mind, as I knew he was watching me place them just so.

This cold fall morning, I see a bushel basket, and it speaks to me: "I'm here, waiting for you to fill me up. See me. Unwanted. Without purpose."

We must never forget that God sees us. He knows when we are empty, alone, and feeling that we are without purpose. He knows what we are capable of, and He is constantly there to fill us up—if we will let Him. If we lean on Him, He will fill us full! *"My cup runneth over."* Psalm 23:5

It can be as simple as saying a little prayer each night when we close our eyes or wake the following day.

It can be as simple as giving thanks before we eat a meal.

It can be as simple as giving a few dollars to someone who needs it.

It can be as simple as loving someone.

It can be as simple as a bushel basket.

Get a bushel basket.

Theo Boyd
Fall 2022

HEAVEN HAS A NEW NURSERY

Death knows no age,
As life becomes an empty stage.
Man, woman, girl, or boy,
The end comes with loss of hope, loss of joy.

As they count ten fingers and ten toes,
Their time won't last, but no one knows.
Precious souls floating in and above,
They need a Grammy, as God gives the love.

They left us through the clouds and skies,
To hear the music of soft lullabies.
The nursery is almost ready and complete,
But help is needed from a heart so sweet.

Heaven has a new nursery—it's filling up fast.
We need someone whose care will last and last.
It's a nursery made for Heaven's perfect little ones,
Someone's daughter, someone's son.

We need someone who loved the military more than most,
Someone whose love spread from coast to coast.
A lady with arms to hold and wrap,
And put them in their cribs for night and nap.

We need someone with lots of steam,
Who'll always be there to cheer their team.
Someone who loved her own children so dear,
To help them feel safe, never fear.

Bethel was her home, until Heaven announced,
Where is the soul to help the babies bounce?
Where is the person who will rock, bottle, and swaddle,
And someone to watch as they grow and toddle?

She's in Texas, the Bethel community,
And we know she'd love this opportunity.
No doubt, she's the best one for the position,
And she would die for this mission.

Heaven has a new nursery, a sacred space,
It's sweet and soft and a pretty place.
Don't worry about this Grammy, so good and nice,
She's in the place they call paradise.

So, the next time you hear that a baby dies,
When everyone is broken down and cries.
You can know she is there, cradling them tight,
And watching them all through the day and the night.

Theo Boyd
In Memory of Patsy Ann Snow
January 2025

SCATTERED HOPE

Hills and valleys stretch across,
Connecting souls found and lost.
The deepest sorrow longs for rest,
As the Scissor-tailed folds her nest.

Finding shade to settle in,
The cattle graze soon to end.
Looking to a sparse collection,
Golden strands of perfection.

Sprinkled forms on open land,
Time to come routinely planned.
Blonde. Bundled. Beautiful. True.
Falling drops while rays break through.

Scared to sink, sorrow the same,
Seasons at play all a game.
Months, years—yielding to cope,
Soaking up scattered hope.

Theo Boyd
Inspired by a field of hay bales, representing HOPE
September 2023

THE NAKED TREE

I feel like the naked tree.
Oh, how can that tree be like me?
As if my skin is gone away,
And all my veins exposed each day.

Raw and brittle in winter's air,
Without shelter in deep despair.
All hope traveling crimson paths,
Left vulnerable to air and may not last.

The bare branches bent and reaching,
As I look at them and what they're teaching.
They stand tall in winds so strong,
And though it is hard—they hold up as long.

Soon, cover will come and warm the heart,
But never forget the deeper part.
Far below—roots hold deep,
And up they sprout for all to reap.

Knowing the truth of its vines,
Helps to pass troubling times.
To let us in and see the source,
a gift for all to chart their course.

The part you see,
Sometimes exposed,
That is its strength,
For all to know.

Oh, how this tree is like me.

Theo Boyd
October 2019

THE COTTON TRAILER

The farmer—genuine, true, sincere,
Working crops from year to year.
Always there to take the call,
Winter, spring, summer, fall.

Toil and time race through the day,
While memories weave to show the way.
Feathering fields, prepared to know,
Wait on each restoring row.

Fields are weeded, grounds are seeded,
Many tools and equipment needed.
But not just a plow, rake, or baler,
What he needs most is his cotton trailer.

Serving proud with a push and pull.
Knowing and ready to soon be full.
Lessening the load he has to make,
Hoping and praying it doesn't break.

Picking and harvest soon is done,
The clouds bring shade from scorching sun.
Wrapped in heart-shaped leaves, today it clings,
Hearing the bells of Heaven ring.

Rushing fast to be the first,
Parched from doubt and drying thirst.
Weathered, worn, but held strong,
Its season here won't be long.

Holding on, but all shall die,
Fibers woven from earth to sky.
Like scattered snow, held in a boll,
Hope carried in his soul.

Our future comes from our past,
It's not about the first bale—but the last.
So, when looking out on fields of cotton,
Remember the trailer and they are not forgotten.

Theo Boyd
In memory of Ronald "Ronnie" Joseph Gerik, Sr.
Christmas 2024

RECIPES FROM MOMMA AND ME

To SAY MOMMA WAS a good host is a vast understatement. She was a machine in the kitchen, while also being the queen of her household. It is rare that I don't picture her either in the laundry room washing, pressing, and sewing clothes or in the kitchen cooking, baking, and preparing food. She always said, "Hobbies make you happy," but taking care of her home and those inside it was far more than a hobby; it was something she prided herself on.

These recipes are a few of my special remembrances of her. They are the parts of my past that take me right back to her kitchen—and right back home.

It isn't so much what's on the table that matters, as what's on the chairs.[19]

—W. S. Gilbert

Nancy Reagan's Pumpkin Pecan Pie[20]

This was our favorite pumpkin pie recipe. Momma would make a pie crust from scratch, but any store-bought pie crust will work. I use foil, loosely tented over the edges, to avoid overbrowning.

4 large eggs

1 can (16 oz.) pumpkin

¾ cup sugar

½ cup dark corn syrup

1 teaspoon ground cinnamon

¼ teaspoon salt

1 unbaked 9-inch pie shell

1 cup pecan halves, left whole or coarsely chopped

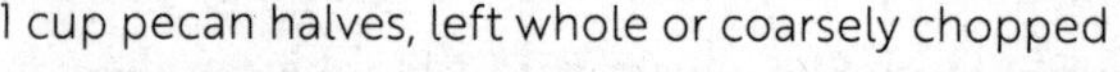

Heat oven to 350 degrees Fahrenheit. In a large bowl, slightly beat the eggs. Stir in remaining filling ingredients until well blended. Pour into the pie shell. Arrange pecans on top. Bake for 50 minutes or until the center is done.

It is the sweet, simple things of life which are the real ones after all.[21]

—Laura Ingalls Wilder

Christmas Cranberry Salad

Momma always poured her mixture into a pretty mold, which she would later turn over onto a crystal plate garnished with lettuce and other greens. Place a dab of whipped topping in the center to make a beautiful centerpiece. I pour mine into one of Momma's beautiful crystal bowls (I'm not as good at the mold thing). Everyone loves this dish!

2 boxes (3 oz. each) raspberry Jell-O

3 cups boiling water

2 cans (14 oz. each) whole cranberry sauce

2 cans (8¼ oz. each) mandarin oranges, drained

1 cup chopped pecans

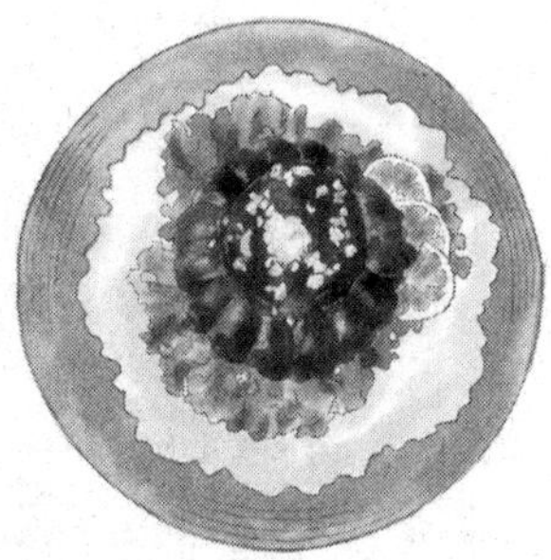

Dissolve the Jell-O gelatin in the water. Add the cranberry sauce, stirring until well blended. Chill until partially set. Add the mandarin oranges and pecans. Mix well. Pour mixture into individual molds (if desired). Chill until set.

Momma's Famous Chocolate Pie

Whew! These chocolate pies were Momma's signature piece. She was known far and wide for this dessert. I always asked her why she shared her recipe with everyone. "Don't you want to keep it a secret?" I'd wonder. She would reply, "It doesn't matter if you give out my recipe—no one can make it like I can." She was right!

Pie Crust Shell

1 cup + 2 tablespoons all-purpose flour

⅓ cup vegetable oil

½ teaspoon salt

2 or 3 tablespoons cold water

Mix the flour, oil, and salt in a bowl until the dough forms particles the size of small peas. Sprinkle in the cold water, 1 tablespoon at a time, mixing until all flour is moistened and the sides of the bowl are almost clean. If your pastry seems dry, add 2 tablespoons oil, not water. If your pastry seems a little too wet, add a little flour. Gather the dough into a ball. Roll out in a circle on a floured surface. Transfer the rolled dough to a 9-inch pie plate. Bake at 400 degrees Fahrenheit for 10–12 minutes or until the crust is slightly browned.

Chocolate Pie Filling

1 cup sugar

6 tablespoons flour

3 tablespoons Hershey's cocoa powder

¼ teaspoon salt

4 egg yolks, beaten

2 cups milk

1 tablespoon butter

1 teaspoon vanilla

In a 2-quart saucepan, mix the sugar, flour, cocoa, and salt together. Add the egg yolks and milk. Cook on medium heat until thick, stirring constantly. Add the butter and vanilla. Pour the chocolate pie filling into the hot crust, right from the oven. There's no need to cool the crust.

Meringue

4 egg whites at room temperature

¼ teaspoon cream of tartar

⅓ cup sugar

Beat the egg whites with the cream of tartar. Add the sugar and beat until stiff peaks form. Spoon the meringue on top of the pie filling. Bake in a 350-degree Fahrenheit oven for twenty minutes or until the meringue turns light brown. Watch this step closely.

Nanny's 5-Minute Fudge

Nanny was my maternal grandmother. She, too, was gifted in the kitchen, but that didn't mean she wouldn't take a shortcut every now and then. This fudge is by far the best I've ever tasted, and it's so easy to make. It will save you time, and the recipe makes quite a bit. Cut into bite-size squares as an after-dinner sweet, or slice it into bigger blocks to wrap and give away. If I can make it, you can too!

⅔ cup evaporated milk

1⅔ cup sugar

½ teaspoon salt

2 cups miniature marshmallows

1½ cups semisweet chocolate chips

1 teaspoon vanilla extract

1 cup chopped nuts (I use pecans)

Mix the evaporated milk, sugar, and salt in a 2-quart saucepan. Heat to boiling over low heat. Boil and stir for 5 minutes. Remove from the heat; add the marshmallows, chocolate chips, vanilla, and nuts, stirring until the marshmallows and chocolate are melted. Pour into a buttered 9x9-inch pan. Refrigerate until firm. When ready to serve, cut into 1½-inch squares.

Friends are like fancy chocolates,
it's what's inside that makes them special.

—Unknown

Lemon Poppy Seed Cake

This is Ronnie Joe's favorite dessert—well, besides a homemade apple pie! He loves the taste of lemon paired with a hint of poppy seed. If he has been out in the field all day, I'll put this cake in his refrigerator as a welcome surprise. I like to put real lemons (whole or wedges) in the middle to add that fresh bit of decoration. I also add a little green accent using a mint leaf to the sides and middle.

Cake

1 box lemon (or white) cake mix

1 box (3.4 oz.) instant lemon pudding mix

½ cup sour cream (or plain yogurt)

1 cup vegetable oil

4 eggs

½ cup water

3 tablespoons poppy seeds

Preheat the oven to 350 degrees Fahreneheit. Spray a Bundt pan with cooking spray (I like the butter-flavored Pam). In a large bowl, mix together with an electric mixer the cake and the pudding mixes. Add the sour cream, oil, eggs, and water. Mix until well blended, about 2 minutes. Do not overmix. Stir in the poppy seeds. Pour the batter into the prepared cake pan. Bake for 40–50 minutes, or until a toothpick inserted in the middle comes out clean. Cool the cake in pan on wire rack for 15 minutes. Then carefully flip cake onto a serving plate. While the cake cools, prepare the glaze.

Glaze

1 cup powdered sugar

1 tablespoon lemon juice

1–2 teaspoons milk

1 teaspoon lemon zest

Lemons and mint leaves, for garnish

Mix ingredients together, adding lemon juice and milk until the consistency is smooth but not too runny. Drizzle the glaze on the cooled cake. Garnish with lemons and mint leaves.

Life needs more slow dances in the kitchen.

—Nikki Allen

Big Red Ice Cream

Big Red is a red cream soda—so rich and so dang good. In the South, Big Red is a common drink on grocery store shelves. But in the North, it can be hard to find. My friends from New York who would visit their grandmother near our farm each summer would always be excited to drink Big Red because they didn't have it where they lived. I always like to keep a two-liter bottle of Big Red on hand to make this ice cream.

3 cans evaporated milk

2 cans Eagle Brand sweetened condensed milk

4–5 cups Big Red soft drink (or other red cream soda)

Chopped strawberries or cherries, optional

Ice cream maker, ice, and rock salt

Mix all ingredients together in an ice cream maker. Follow the instructions for your machine, adding ice and rock salt to the sides. Turn the machine on and get ready to enjoy the best ice cream you've ever had! Add chopped strawberries or cherries, if you like.

Ice cream is a sweet reminder of childhood.

—Unknown

Snow Ice Cream

Momma always froze this ice cream first, and then we could eat it later, once it hardened. I love snow ice cream!

1 cup milk

⅓ cup sugar

1 teaspoon vanilla extract

Dash of salt

8 cups clean snow*

In a large bowl, whisk the milk, sugar, vanilla, and salt together. Scoop up some fresh snow (about 8 cups) and immediately stir it into the milk mixture until it reaches a good, creamy consistency.

*Make sure this is clean, white snow—not yellow!

Memories of Momma in the kitchen are always sweet.

—Theo Boyd

Momma's Perfect Peanut Patties

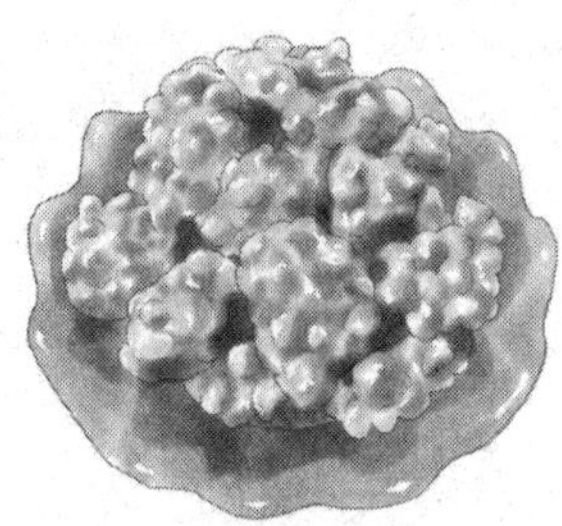

2 cups sugar

½ cup water

Dash of salt

½ cup light Karo syrup

1½ cups raw peanuts

1 tablespoon butter

1 teaspoon vanilla extract

2–3 drops red food coloring

In a 2-quart glass measuring bowl, microwave the sugar, water, salt, and Karo syrup for 3 minutes. Stir and add the peanuts. Microwave for an additional 10 minutes or until the mixture reaches the soft ball stage of candy-making. Remove the bowl from the microwave and add the butter, vanilla, and food coloring. Once it's cool, beat the mixture until it's creamy. Drop by tablespoonfuls onto a greased cookie sheet or pour the entire mixture onto a greased pizza pan for one large peanut patty.

Divinity Candy

Divinity candy-making almost takes divine intervention! I remember many times when I had to throw away the bowl, the spatula, *and* the mixer because my divinity turned into concrete. But follow the recipe closely, pray hard, and enjoy yourself some divinity!

2 cups sugar

⅓ cup water

⅓ cup light corn syrup

Healthy dash of salt

2 egg whites

1 teaspoon vanilla extract

½ cup chopped pecans

1 cup whole pecan halves (for decoration)

Combine the sugar, water, corn syrup, and salt in a 2-quart glass bowl. Cover with plastic wrap and microwave on high for 5 minutes. Remove the bowl from the microwave and remove the plastic wrap. Stir well and return the bowl to the microwave uncovered. Cook on high for another 4–5 minutes until it has reached the hard ball stage of candy-making. Remove and cool about 4 minutes. Beat the egg whites with a mixer until stiff peaks form. Pour the sugar mixture over the egg whites, beating constantly with a mixer until mixture starts to lose its gloss and holds together, about 4–5 minutes. Stir in the vanilla and pecans. Drop by tablespoons onto wax paper. Add 1 pecan half to each drop.

But the only way to find out is to try.

—Laura Ingalls Wilder

Theo's Christmas Punch

There are so many ways to dress up this punch. You can freeze cranberries inside ice cube trays to add to the punch. You can also add rosemary or mint sprigs to each glass. I like to slice oranges very thinly and lay those near the center of the punch bowl.

½ cup sugar

1 teaspoon ground cinnamon

1 teaspoon ground nutmeg

Dash of salt

2 cups boiling water

2 bottles (16 oz. each) cranberry juice cocktail

2 cans (6 oz. each) frozen pineapple juice concentrate

2 bottles (12 oz. each) club soda

Ice cubes, optional

In a small mixing bowl, stir together the sugar, cinnamon, nutmeg, and salt. Pour the boiling water over the mixture. Stir until the sugar is dissolved. Chill in the refrigerator for about 20 minutes. When you're ready to serve the punch, pour it into a punch bowl. Add the remaining ingredients, and ice cubes, if desired.

Tonight, punch;
Tomorrow, brunch.
—Theo Boyd

NOTES

1. "A Harvest of Friends," *Little House on the Prairie* (Michael Landon and Ed Friendly, Executive Producers, NBC Studios, 1974–1983).
2. Lisa M. Shulman, adapted from *Before and After Loss: A Neurologist's Perspective on Loss, Grief, and Our Brain* (Johns Hopkins University Press, 2018).
3. Theo Boyd, *My Grief Is Not Like Yours* (Forefront Books, 2023), p. 28.
4. Paula McClain, QuoteFancy, https://quotefancy.com/quote/1538025/Paula-McLain-You-have-to-digest-life-You-have-to-chew-it-up-and-love-it-all-through.
5. Linda Ellis, "The Dash" from *Live Your Dash: Make Every Moment Matter* (Sterling Ethos, 2014).
6. Sung by Jimmy Durante on the album *Jimmy Durante's Way of Life* (Warner Bros. Records, 1965); written by Sammy Cahn and Julie Styne.
7. Attributed to Mark Twain, https://www.goodreads.com/quotes/505050-the-two-most-important-days-in-your-life-are-the.
8. Theo Boyd, *My Grief Is Not Like Yours* (Forefront Books, 2023), pp. 118–119.
9. Laura Ingalls Wilder, *The Long Winter* (HarperCollins, 1953).
10. Poison, "Every Rose Has Its Thorn," from the album *Open Up and Say . . . Ahh!* (Capitol Records, 1988).

11. Eben Alexander, MD, *Proof of Heaven: A Neurosurgeon's Journey into the Afterlife* (Simon & Schuster, 2012).
12. Brian Lawlor, "What Is Hope and Why Do We Need It?" *Global Brain Health Institute*, December 30, 2022.
13. Clara H. Scott, "Open My Eyes That I May See," https://hymnary.org/text/open_my_eyes_that_i_may_see.
14. John F. Walvoord, Editor, *The Bible Knowledge Commentary: New Testament* (David C. Cook, 1983).
15. Robert Lightner, *Angels, Satan, and Demons* (W Pub Group, 1998), p. 166.
16. Florida Georgia Line, "Dirt," from the album *Anything Goes* (Republic Nashville, 2014).
17. Florida Georgia Line, "Dirt."
18. Readily available and adapted from the poem by George Ella Lyon, "Where I'm From," http://www.georgeellalyon.com/where.html.
19. W. S. Gilbert, https://quotefancy.com/quote/1206168/W-S-Gilbert-It-isn-t-so-much-what-s-on-the-table-that-matters-as-what-s-on-the-chairs.
20. https://www.food.com/recipe/nancy-reagans-easy-pumpkin-pecan-pie-181046.
21. Attributed to Laura Ingalls Wilder, https://www.brainyquote.com/quotes/laura_ingalls_wilder_126425.

ABOUT THE AUTHOR

Thelizabeth "Theo" Boyd was born and raised on a farm in Whitney, Texas, and was named after her grandmothers Thelma and Elizabeth. Known as "Theo" since middle school, she began writing poems with her father and learning resilience from her mother. She pursued higher education later in life, becoming a high school English and creative writing teacher—earning "Rookie Teacher of the Year" her first year—and contributing as a newspaper columnist.

In 2019, Theo experienced a traumatic loss that inspired her debut memoir, *My Grief Is Not Like Yours*, and launched her podcast, *Think Theo*, where she explores the complexities of grief. Since the book's release in May 2023, Theo has been featured on numerous media outlets, including *Newsweek*, *The Sun*, and *The Daily Mail*, and has received seventeen national and international book awards, including the Indie Excellence Award, two Global Book Awards, and the 2025 Texas Rising Lone Star Author Award.

When not writing or speaking, Theo enjoys farm life with her dog, Manly, as they build their new home. She is passionate about helping others navigate grief, using both personal stories and national research to offer hope and healing, and has recently become a Certified Grief Educator.

NOTES PAGES

Enjoyed this book? Dive deeper.

Download Theo Boyd's exclusive research study at: www.stateofgrief.com

Gain access to bonus insights and data from Theo's national study, *The Silent Weight of Grief in America.*